Mastering Financial Accounting Essentials

Founded in 1807, John Wiley & Sons is the oldest independent publishing company in the United States. With offices in North America, Europe, Australia and Asia, Wiley is globally committed to developing and marketing print and electronic products and services for our customers' professional and personal knowledge and understanding.

The Wiley Finance series contains books written specifically for finance and investment professionals as well as sophisticated individual investors and their financial advisors. Book topics range from portfolio management to e-commerce, risk management, financial engineering, valuation and financial instrument analysis, as well as much more.

For a list of available titles, please visit our Web site at www.WileyFinance.com.

Mastering Financial Accounting Essentials

The Critical Nuts and Bolts

STUART A. McCRARY

WILEY

John Wiley & Sons, Inc.

Published by John Wiley & Sons, Inc., Hoboken, New Jersey.
Published simultaneously in Canada.

For general information on our other products and services or for technical support, please
contact our Customer Care Department within the United States at (800) 762-2974, outside
the United States at (317) 572-3993 or fax (317) 572-4002.

Wiley also publishes its books in a variety of electronic formats. Some content that appears in
print may not be available in electronic books. For more information about Wiley products,
visit our web site at www.wiley.com.

Library of Congress Cataloging-in-Publication Data:

McCrary, Stuart A.
  Mastering financial accounting essentials : the critical nuts and bolts /
Stuart A. McCrary.
      p. cm. – (Wiley finance series)
  Includes index.
  ISBN 978-0-470-39332-1 (cloth)
  1. Accounting. 2. Financial statements. I. Title.
  HF5636.M42 2010
  657–dc22
                                                    2009017159

Printed in the United States of America

10 9 8 7 6 5 4 3 2 1

To my loving wife, Nancy

Contents

Preface

Most accounting textbooks are written to teach accounting to future accountants, the creators of financial statements. This book is intended to explain financial accounting to company managers and investors, the users of financial statements. As a result, this book will give an intuitive understanding of the accounting process and standard accounting reports. This text does not focus on accounting rules and therefore is not intended to teach accounting to future accountants.

The questions at the end of each chapter follow an extended example of a new company being created. As the company is created and grows, new kinds of activities require accountants to record a widening variety of business transactions. The questions follow the topic in each chapter and don't necessarily appear in chronological order. However, a list of accounting entries sums up the year in chronological order.

The book is written as a text for an executive master's program in business school or part of the business curriculum in a professional degree program (engineering, law, medicine, etc.). To respect the scarce time of the student, the most important material will occupy the main text. Students can read the chapters without studying the questions at the end of the chapter, but they should work through both the chapters and questions for a better understanding of the material.

Not every accounting student is enthusiastic about having to learn accounting. Yet they attend the class because modern business makes it important for everyone outside the accounting department to understand the company's accounting system.

Perhaps it would be more rewarding to start over and build a logical accounting system from scratch. If no accounting system existed, we could design it to meet the needs of a modern business, to be logical, and to be understandable. But this text must describe our existing accounting system to be useful to the reader. The reader will discover that the existing accounting system is logical and does meet the needs of modern business.

Traditional accounting textbooks are much easier to understand if the reader already has a good grasp of accounting concepts. A reader without prior knowledge may need to read a traditional accounting text twice because material in the early chapters is clear only after the reader is familiar with content in other parts of the book. This text will seek to present the material in a way that explains the key features of modern accounting step by step and will develop an intuitive understanding of accounting.

Although this text will not invent a new accounting system, it will introduce the concepts of modern accounting in an orderly way that sounds a bit like the evolution of a primitive system into our current practices. This text will start with a limited accounting system that does not include many key features of modern accounting. These features (such as accrual accounting, which can make accounting numbers more useful for business decisions) are successively added, so the reader can understand how these features work and why they are used.

Disclaimer: Financial accounting textbooks generally do not include a disclaimer. These textbooks are published to educate students interested in becoming accountants or to be an authoritative source on accounting rules and methods. As explained in the Forward, this text is not written to educate future accountants or to serve as a thorough summary of accounting rules. Instead, the book serves to explain accounting to individuals who interact with accountants and accounting records. This text should not be used to determine how financial statements should be prepared.

The text begins with the assumption that the reader is not familiar with any accounting jargon and is not familiar with double-entry accounting. Accounting concepts are introduced along with the language accountants use to describe the process. The name of a particular account (such as ASSETS or CASH) will be written in uppercase to make it clear when the text describes that account. Gradually, the main accounting statements are described using the previously introduced accounting vocabulary. In this way, the reader learns about accounting without having to have a grounding in the topic, then gets to rehearse the language used by accountants.

Later chapters describe how businesses and users can assess the usefulness of accounting records, reduce the opportunity for fraud, and to use accounting information intelligently.

Each chapter presents key accounting concepts. Questions at the end of each chapter revisit these key concepts by reviewing how accountants handle common business transactions, with answers at the back of the book. The descriptions are short by design and some readers may want to read more if they need to know more about particular topics not thoroughly covered, such as valuing intangible assets, leasing, pension fund accounting, accounting for subsidiaries, accounting for nondollar transactions, stock options, or partnership accounting.

April 2009   Stuart A. McCrary

Acknowledgments

I would like to thank the many people at Chicago Partners LLC (a division of Navigant Consulting, Inc.) for their insights on presenting this accounting curriculum simply. In particular, I thank George Minkovsky for making a careful reading of the text.

I also want to thank my students and the administration of Northwestern University, especially program directors Walter B. Herbst and Richard M. Lueptow. This book reflects my efforts to create an executive master's curriculum that covers financial accounting in an incredibly short period. This book reflects our mutual efforts to present essential accounting information to nonaccountants so that these students can become more effect business leaders.

CHAPTER 1

Creating Ledger Accounting

If we set out to create the modern system of accounting, we would start with a goal. Our accounting system is a measuring and monitoring system, so we set as a goal to count the things that matter to a business and report the results in a way that is helpful to the managers. This chapter takes an important first step in providing a systematic way to count and organize business data.

We could start with a primitive counting system using rocks and a clay urn. This is not a history of accounting, but this text will make reference to how primitive record keeping can be used to account for business transactions. The history of accounting is complex, and this text will not try to tell that story. However, these early accounting tools can provide the student with an understanding of why accounting methods evolved.

We could use the urn to contain a count of some product our company owns. If our retro business were importing and selling myrrh, we would add pebbles to the urn every time a ship came in from distant lands with a supply of myrrh. Each time we sold some myrrh, we would remove pebbles from the urn. At every point in time, the urn would contain our count of the stock of myrrh on hand.

Of course, our business may buy and sell many different products. We would need another urn for every product we want to count.

We could also devote an urn to the amount of debt we owe. If our currency were gold coins, we would record one pebble in the urn for each gold coin owed to our lenders. We may need to use smaller pebbles for the debt account, so there is room in the urn. The size of the pebble doesn't matter much because we really have to count the pebbles each time we want to see how much money we owe.

Urns could help the smallest of businesses to keep track of their business, but urns are unwieldy as the number of items we need to count grows. In addition, we do not know the count in the urn at any previous point unless we write down the count somewhere else and preserve the information outside of our counting system. Finally, when we count the pebbles and the thing we are tracking, we have no way to distinguish theft from human error in updating the pebbles in the urn.

We can fix all of these problems by making the count a little differently. If we have the clay to make urns, we might want to build a clay tablet to count our myrrh, our debt, and anything else worth counting. One system would use soft clay tablets and a blunt-tipped stick. Each time we buy more myrrh, we etch a "tally mark" into the clay.

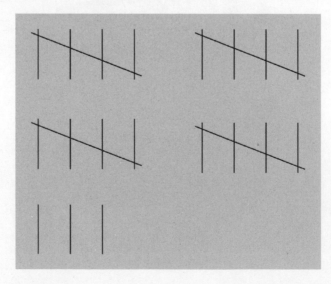

The previous system allowed us to count decreases to our stock of myrrh as easily as increases. Unlike the hard clay urn, this tablet does not easily let us indicate that previous inventory has been sold. If we were using clay urns to count our myrrh, we could pull pebbles out of the urn as we sold myrrh to our customers. To be as useful as a clay urn, we would need to count the number of units of myrrh we acquired and the number we sold. The next drawing shows a representation of how the soft clay tablets can be adapted to count both increases and decreases in the amount of myrrh on hand.

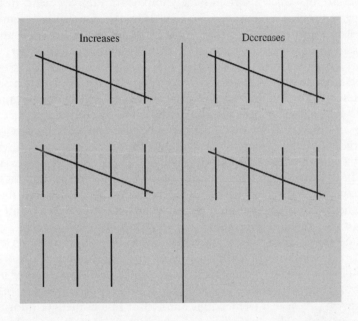

The flat stone covering a tomb or grave is called a ledger (*Random House Unabridged Dictionary of the English Language*, 1966). Perhaps this stone lends its name to the soft clay tablets used to count the assets and liabilities of this old world business. According to the New York State Society of CPAs (www.nysscpa.org), assets are defined as "an economic resource that is expected to be of benefit in the future" and liabilities are defined as the "DEBTS or obligations owed by one entity (debtor) to another entity (creditor) payable in money, goods, or services."

This clay tablet containing tallies has a couple advantages over rocks and urns. We can indicate our location on the ledger at certain points in time, such as at month-end and year-end. When we fill out a tablet, we can let it dry in the sun and preserve a record of our counting procedure. In addition, we may be able to count our stock of goods with fewer, more compact resources (tablets are smaller than most clay urns). Also, we can quickly see a running total of these products in our accounting records.

The next improvement over the clay tablet method is to record the tally marks on paper. Today, paper is an inexpensive material and much lighter than clay tablets. It is a small step from etching tally marks in a soft clay tablet to inking tally marks on a piece of paper. Although less durable than clay, we can introduce a second hugely important improvement. Instead of counting the myrrh as one tally per unit of myrrh, we can use numbers to represent quantities. This is important if we are willing to sell anything other than standard units of myrrh. Relying on numbers and paper, we can be much more precise in our counting.

The other feature that a paper ledger permits is to count the assets and liabilities in currency units instead of physical quantities. For certain kinds of assets and liabilities, this is not a change. The liabilities described as the number of gold coins we owe a lender are denominated in currency. If we count the number of oranges we hold and the number of apples, we can't directly compare the count because they are as different as apples and oranges. If we instead describe the value of the apples and the oranges instead of the count, then we can make intelligent comparisons between the apple count and the orange count and we can even accumulate assets into larger subtotals with meaningful results.

Students who are new to accounting may conclude that accountants don't care how many apples or how many oranges we own. Of course, this physical count can be tremendously important, but it doesn't enter into the primary account ledger or standard accounting reports. Modern information systems preserve a tremendous amount of this nonledger information, which doesn't usually appear on published financial statements. However, this text and most other accounting texts focus primarily on the value of the transactions and very little on physical quantities.

COUNT EVERYTHING

So far, it is not clear what assets and what liabilities we should count. The short answer, of course, is that we should count all of them. This is a challenging task, and the bulk of this text describes how accountants keep track of business transactions. It is important to count all assets and all liabilities because we live in a world where there is considerable pressure to disclose financial information to investors and creditors. More fundamentally, if we

TABLE 1.1 Impact of Changes in Asset and Liability Values

Type of Entry	Impact on Equity
Increase assets	Increase equity
Decrease assets	Decrease equity
Increase liabilities	Decrease equity
Decrease liabilities	Increase equity

have accurately counted all our assets and all our liabilities, we can net the two to see "how we are doing." If assets greatly exceed our liabilities, we have equity (defined as the "residual interest in the assets of an entity that remains after deducting its liabilities" (www.nysscpa.org/prof_library/guide.htm#e)) or net worth in the business. If we don't (or can't) count every asset and liability, we can't really know how much the assets exceed the liabilities (if at all).

So far, we have been counting only assets and liabilities. While it may appear to be unnecessary to count our equity, it certainly would be possible to do so. One way to count the equity is to realize that any increase in assets (all other things being equal) increases our equity or makes us richer by an equal amount. Likewise, a decrease in assets (again, all other things being equal) decreases our equity by the same amount. Similarly, an increase in liabilities makes us poorer (lowers our equity) and a decrease in a liability increases an equity account. A list of some of the combinations appears in Table 1.1.

THE BEGINNINGS OF DOUBLE-ENTRY ACCOUNTING

If we count all the assets and liabilities, accountants can directly measure the benefit of a transaction. Suppose a merchant sells myrrh that costs 5 gold coins in return for 10 gold coins. The currency account increases by 10 gold coins (an asset), so our net worth increases by the same 10 gold coins. Our inventory of myrrh decreases by 5 gold coins, so the net worth declines by 5 gold coins. The net of the two transactions (which actually occur simultaneously) is to increase the firm equity by 5 gold coins.

Of course, as shown in Table 1.1, the imputed matching of transactions with changes in equity is frequently not an actual accounting reality but does offer a perspective on the link among assets, liabilities, and

TABLE 1.2 Some Combinations of Business Transactions

Type of Transaction	Offsetting Transaction	Example
Increase asset	Decrease a different asset	Use cash to acquire an asset
Increase asset	Decrease a different asset	Sell used tools for cash
Increase liability	Increase asset	Borrow money to buy asset
Decrease liability	Decrease asset	Use cash to pay off a debt
Increase liability	Decrease liability	Issue bond to repay bank loan

equity. In the preceding sales transaction, it is also useful to think of the mismatched change in assets (decrease in the value of myrrh in inventory by 5 gold coins versus an increase in currency of 10 gold coins). It is no accident that the mismatched change in assets exactly matches the change in equity.

It will soon be obvious if we commit to count everything (including an explicit account of the equity), that every counting transaction requires at least two entries. In addition to the types of matched transactions in Table 1.2, several other types of transactions are possible. Chapters 3 through 5 will describe these transactions.

Table 1.2 does not contain an exhaustive list of exchanges that are possible. Also, the value of the two transactions does not always match, so there can be a third or more entries required to describe a business transaction. When the values of the transactions do not match, the increase or decrease in the value of the firm absorbs the difference, as with the sale of myrrh discussed earlier.

Double-entry accounting merely recognizes that any need to count some transaction in the business creates the need to count at least one additional offsetting transaction. Further, if all the entries are matched with entries to equity, the offsetting equity amount not only describes the net benefit or detriment to the firm but also quantifies the net entry required to complete the description of the transaction.

Note that modern accounting does follow the pattern of matching each change in asset and liability with a change in equity but in a way that will be described in Chapters 4 and 5. After we add a few more features to our accounting system, the receipt of 10 gold coins will be instead matched with an equal entry called SALES, and the reduction in inventory that cost 5 gold coins will be paired with a 5-gold-coin entry called COST OF GOODS. These are called temporary accounts that will be netted and reclassified as equity at some point in the future.

DOUBLE-ENTRY RECORDING OF BUSINESS TRANSACTIONS

As stated earlier, the value of the company equity can be calculated as the excess value, if any, of the assets of a company over the value of the liabilities, as in Equation 1.1.

It is convenient to rearrange Equation 1.1 to become Equation 1.2 using standard algebra:

$$\text{Assets} - \text{Liabilities} = \text{Equity} \qquad (1.1)$$

$$\text{Assets} = \text{Liabilities} + \text{Equity} \qquad (1.2)$$

Equation 1.2 demonstrates that the assets of the firm are owned by two groups. The liabilities represent lenders to the company, and the equity holders owned the excess over the value of the liabilities. Equation 1.2 represents the accountant's view of the ownership of the company, and double-entry accounting is a system to count or account for that ownership.

Returning to the system of clay tablets, double-entry can be viewed as a way of keeping track of the equity of the company. Instead of tallies, record numbers that increase the value of equity on the right-hand side of the clay tablet. Record the assets on the left. Record the liabilities on the right-hand side, too, because clay tablets do not accommodate negative numbers or subtraction very well.

Returning to Equation 1.2, the value of assets equals the value of the liabilities and equity. Because this is true both before and after each new transaction, it must also be true of individual transactions. This balance between assets, liabilities, and equity is one of the fundamental constraints of double-entry accounting. While it poses a challenge to the student who is new to accounting, it also provides a valuable cross-check to make sure: (1) that everything has been counted and (2) that they are counted in a way to preserve the match in Equations 1.1 and 1.2.

HANDLING DEBITS AND CREDITS

Using Equation 1.2 as a model, we could set up a clay tablet accordingly. Tallies to asset accounts (entries for assets as they are acquired) would occur on the left column. Tallies to liabilities assumed would be placed on the right-hand column. Similarly, tallies for equity would be placed on the right-hand column. Furthermore, the number of tallies in the asset column must match the number of tallies for liabilities and equity combined.

Following the preceding pattern, a reduction in assets gets tallied separately from increases in assets. So tallies for increases in assets get posted to the left column and tallies for decreases in assets get posted to the right column. Because increases to liabilities get posted on the right, decreases to liabilities get posted on the left column. Similarly, increases to equity get posted on the right, so decreases get posted on the left.

In a double-entry system, transactions are generally recorded in one of two columns. Accountants use the word *debit* to describe an entry on the left column and *credit* to describe an entry on the right column. Just like sailors who use *port* and *starboard* to describe left and right, the two accounting words mean little more than left and right.

The way accountants handle the debits and credits does matter. The paper ledger needs to convey whether a particular transaction increases or decreases the asset, liability, or equity. Several alternatives are possible, but accountants have developed the following rules:

- A debit entry for an asset reports an increase to that account.
- A credit entry for an asset reports a decrease to that account.
- A debit entry for a liability reports a decrease to that account.
- A credit entry for a liability reports an increase to that account.
- A debit entry for equity reports a decrease to that account.
- A credit entry for equity reports an increase to that account.

Using this list of rules, the accountant knows how to accumulate the impact of these accounting transactions. Notice that the assumptions are the same for liabilities and equity but opposite for assets. Assets = liabilities + equity both before and after an individual accounting transaction is included. It follows that any increase (debit) in an asset must be paired with an equal decrease (credit) to another asset (e.g., buying inventory with cash), or an increase (credit) to either a liability or equity account. The size of the debits exactly equals the size of the credits.

The accountant's primary job is to tally the impact of these individual accounting entries for each asset, liability, and equity. However, by defining the meaning of debits and credits according to the list above, the accountant has a cross-check to identify whether all entries appear to have been included in the data correctly. If the sum of the debits equals the sum of the credits, the accounts are "in balance."

If the accounts are "out of balance," debits do not match credits and something is wrong. But if the accounts are in balance, the accounting entries could still be wrong. For example, both a debit and matching credit could be missing. Or both the debit and credit could be incorrectly included in duplicate. Or the wrong account may have been used.

KEEPING TRACK OF DATA

Modern accounting systems do not use clay urns, soft tablets, or even paper ledgers. Instead, companies store accounting inputs in databases that may bear no resemblance to urns, tablets, or ledger paper. Accounting textbooks, however, like to display accounting information in ways that resemble the antiquated technologies.

The T-account chronicles what was placed on a sheet of ledger paper. In paper-based accounting, each account (CASH, INVENTORY, etc.) has a separate sheet of paper with columns for increases and decreases to the account. The columns resemble the earliest method of accounting with clay urns and pebbles, except that the paper can reflect currency.

Following is an example of a merchant who begins with 15 gold coins, buys 10 units of myrrh at 1 gold coin each, and sells 1 unit of myrrh at 2 gold coins in the marketplace. The T-accounts for these transactions are presented in Figure 1.1.

When a computer is used to keep track of the transactions, the T-account is unwieldy. Instead, just the transaction details are recorded. For example, the same transactions are included in the list in Table 1.3.

A MATHEMATICAL DESCRIPTION OF DOUBLE-ENTRY CONVENTIONS

Students new to accounting may find it helpful to think of accounting as a mathematical system. An alternative set of rules for recording transactions appears in Table 1.4.

Under this system, you may post an increase to an asset such as EQUIPMENT together with a decrease in an asset such as CASH (i.e., the company bought the equipment with cash). The entry to EQUIPMENT would be a positive number and the entry to CASH would be a negative number reflecting the same amount of cash. Or you may post an increase to an asset such as EQUIPMENT together with an increase in a liability like ACCOUNTS

Cash		Inventory		Equity	
15					15
	10	10			
2		1			1

FIGURE 1.1 T-Accounts of Myrrh Transactions

TABLE 1.3   General Journal

Account	Debit	Credit
Cash	15	
Equity		15
Inventory	10	
Cash		10
Cash	2	
Inventory		1
Equity		1

PAYABLE. Under this coding system, the increases in the EQUIPMENT account may be entered as positive numbers, and both the decrease in CASH and the increase in ACCOUNTS PAYABLE could be recorded as a negative. Under this coding system, a complete set of entries describing a transaction would always sum to zero.

In fact, accountants go to great lengths to avoid using negative numbers. Probably bookkeeping conventions were developed so that staff did not need to perform subtraction very often. Accounting software programs generally

TABLE 1.4   An Alternative to the Debit-Credit System for Recording Business Transactions

Conventional	Example	Alternative
Record (positive) asset amounts in the left (debit) column.	A company receives cash.	Record positive asset amounts in a single column.
Record a decrease in asset amounts in the right (credit) column.	The company sells some land it had owned.	Record negative asset amounts in a single column.
Record (positive) liability amounts in the right (credit) column.	The company borrows money from a bank.	Record negative liability amounts in a single column.
Record a decrease in liability amounts in the left (debit) column.	The company repays money to a bank.	Record positive liability amounts in a single column.
Record (positive) equity amounts in the right (debit) column.	The company sells new shares of stock.	Record negative equity amounts in a single column.
Record a decrease in equity amounts in the left (debit) column.	The company pays a dividend.	Record positive equity amounts in a single column.

do not carry debits or credits as negative values. In any case, collapsing the debit and credit columns into one column with positive or negative numbers would be reinventing the double-entry system. In order to understand the way accountants think, it is therefore important to understand how accountants use debits and credits to avoid using negative numbers.

HANDLING INCOME ITEMS

The simple accounting model we have does not yet include accounts like SALES, REVENUES, COST OF GOODS SOLD, or INTEREST EXPENSE. Chapter 4 introduces these accounts. It is still possible to account for all these business transactions, although the method described here would not be acceptable to a modern business for several reasons. The rest of this chapter will describe how this very simple system lays the foundation for a system capable of describing a wide range of transactions. This explanation will also highlight the advantages of adding important features present in a modern accounting system.

We already showed how sales of myrrh could be recorded or journaled as changes in the asset accounts (cash and myrrh inventory) along with equity. The same method could be used for all the revenues and expenses of a business.

DETERMINING PROFIT IN THE SIMPLE ACCOUNTING MODEL

Modern accounting systems do have revenue and expense accounts. Our simple system can reveal whether the company is profitable. Using the counting method employed so far, all the revenues and expenses are instead entered as increases or decreases in net worth or equity. To determine the profit over a period of time such as three months or a year, compare the equity at the beginning of the period with the equity at the end of the period. Of course, if the business has other types of transactions affecting the equity of the company (such as the sale of stock or payment of dividends), the net income would equal the change in equity less the impact of these sources and uses of equity.

PERMANENT ACCOUNTS OVERVIEW

All of the asset, liability, and equity accounts are called permanent accounts. In our primitive accounting system and in modern accounting, the value in each account reflects the accumulation of all activity. The value of cash in a bank account reflects a zero starting balance (perhaps starting years ago) plus all the deposits and all the withdrawals. So the cash balance at a particular point in time includes the net impact of all activities since the inception of the business.

Although accountants accumulate all the transactions affecting each account, they present the results at a particular point in time. The year-end balance sheet (described in Chapter 3) presents the asset, liability, and equity accounts from the beginning of the company to that year-end date.

TEMPORARY ACCOUNTS OVERVIEW

The preceding method of calculating income works because it is possible to calculate the value of permanent accounts at different points in time. The equity as of the third quarter includes all equity entries from the inception of the company to the end of the third quarter. Similarly, the equity as of the fourth quarter includes all the equity entries from the inception of the company to the end of the fourth quarter. The difference between these two totals equals the entries made to equity during the fourth quarter.

Business managers and investors are interested in results during a quarter or year. In Chapter 4, we introduce temporary accounts that account for revenues and expenses over an interval. These accounts are reset to zero at the end of each accounting period, which is why they are called temporary accounts. In addition to totaling the change in equity over a shorter period, we will also add a number of accounts to measure the reasons for the change in equity. The resulting income statement will provide considerably more information about why the company made money. The revenue and expense accounts such as SALES, INTEREST EXPENSE, RENT, and TAXES are examples of these temporary accounts.

CONCLUSION

Double-entry accounting was developed to count business transactions centuries ago. Accounting techniques evolved as businesses grew and became more complicated, but the same general rules and conventions support modern accounting. The process begins by recording business transactions as debits and credits into a number of accounts. Then, these transactions are combined by account to create the balance sheet and income statements. This process and analysis of the completed statements is described in the chapters that follow.

Note: For each of the questions that follow, show how the business transaction would be handled by accountants. In each case, show the accounts that would reflect the transactions, the dollar amount of the transactions the accountants would record, and whether the entry is a debit or credit.

1.1. You work for Lavalier Corporation. During the past several years, you have been working with the company to develop new communication technologies. Based primarily on your efforts, the company has acquired several valuable patents. The company has decided that the most attractive way of commercializing these patents is to set up a new company and provide you with a substantial equity stake in the business. Lavalier company lawyers have created a U.S. "C" corporation (the standard U.S. corporate structure) named Lavalier Communications, Inc. (LCI). Late in 20X0, the new company created a board of directors from senior officers in Lavalier Corporation and several independent (outside) directors. On January 2, 20X1, the board of directors met and named you president and chief operating officer (COO) of the new company. The board also named the corporate treasurer of Lavalier Corporation as the chairman and chief executive officer (CEO). The board of directors authorized 5 million shares of common stock ($1 par value). On January 2, 20X1, Lavalier transferred $5 million to a newly established bank account at First National Bank in return for 1 million shares of common stock (par value $1 per share).

1.2. On January 2, 20X1, the board of LCI also granted you options to buy 200,000 shares of stock at $5 per share expiring in five years. The options may be exercised (i.e., you can exchange the options plus $5 per share for common stock) at any point after three years up to expiration in five years.

1.3. Based on prior discussions, the bank immediately moved $2 million into a 5 percent bond maturing 12/31/X3. The remaining funds remain in a demand deposit account earning a floating rate of interest.

1.4. On January 2, 20X1, as agreed in the December Lavalier Corporation board meeting, LCI acquires key patents from Lavalier Bermuda PLC for $2 million.

1.5. On January 16, you lease office space for one year at a nearby office park for $4,000 per month beginning in February. On January 16, you make a security deposit of one month's rent and pay the first month's rent. Additional rent payments are due on the first day of each month beginning March 1. Show entries through March.

1.6. On January 19, you buy miscellaneous office equipment totaling $45,000. Your vendor expects payment in 45 days to avoid finance charges of 1¼ percent per month, so you pay on 2/27/X1.

1.7. On January 28, you contract with a multinational custom manufacturer to produce 10,000 new communication devices (NCDs) per month. They will ship you 5,000 in June, then 10,000 per month after that for a net delivered price of $10 per unit. The manufacturer asks you to make a one-time advance payment for the first three months' supply to provide them with part of the funding for setting up the new manufacturing process.

1.8. You receive 5,000 NCDs on June 19.

1.9. You receive 10,000 NCDs on July 23.

1.10. You receive 10,000 NCDs on August 22.

1.11. You receive 10,000 NCDs on September 19. You pay the contract manufacturer 7 days later.

1.12. You receive 10,000 NCDs on October 22. You pay the invoice amount (at $10/unit) immediately.

1.13. You receive 10,000 NCDs on November 21. You pay the invoice amount (at $10/unit) immediately.

1.14. You receive 10,000 NCDs on December 21. You pay the invoice amount (at $10/unit) immediately.

CHAPTER 2

Accounting Conventions

The modern accounting system follows a number of basic principles and conventions. This chapter will interrupt the description of basic accounting methods to explore these principles and conventions much like an extended glossary. The reader may wish to read this information after reviewing later chapters on the balance sheet, income statement, and other basic topics.

REASONS ACCOUNTANTS DEVELOP CONVENTIONS

Accountants sometimes make assumptions or employ methods to make accounting numbers more useful to the readers of financial statements. Often, the choice of assumptions or methods is beyond the control of the company. For example, the company may have no ability to decide whether to list a particular item in the financial statements, in the footnotes, or not at all. In many cases, standards promulgated by the Financial Accounting Standards Board (FASB), the U.S. Securities and Exchange Commission (SEC), the Internal Revenue Service (IRS), or the American Institute of Certified Public Accountants (AICPA) dictate how financial statements are prepared.

In other cases, companies have choices that can affect the published financial results. For example, companies may decide how to value inventory and how to handle depreciation. Chapter 3 describes the first-in, first-out (FIFO) method and the last-in, first-out (LIFO) method. Chapter 5 describes the straight-line method of depreciation and two alternatives.

Accounting conventions include the choices and assumptions made in preparing the financial statements.

ACCOUNTING CYCLE

The accounting cycle is typically one year. An accounting cycle may not equal one year for newly formed companies or companies changing the ending date of their fiscal year.

The cycle begins with accounts on the income statement carrying balances of zero. At the end of the fiscal year for the company, an income statement is developed, then the balances in the accounts on the income statement are adjusted back to zero. The process of adjusting these accounts back to zero is called "closing."

Companies usually produce quarterly financial statements. From these statements, it may appear that a company has a quarterly accounting cycle, but most companies do not close the books on these quarterly dates.

CLASSIFICATION

Classification refers to the way business transactions are entered in the accounting records of the firm. Entries are classified as ASSET, LIABILITY, EQUITY, REVENUE, or EXPENSE. Each of these five types of accounts contains many specific accounts. Accountants should classify similar accounts in a consistent way.

COMPARABILITY

The way accounting statements are prepared should be similar over time. The same accounting conventions should generally be used from one year to the next so that differences between years reflect company transactions, not changes in accounting assumptions.

Companies are permitted to change accounting conventions. However, companies should document the impact of changing standards in statements prior to the change.

CONSERVATISM

When a question arises, accountants argue for the alternative that shows lower income or lower values for assets, or both. This point requires some clarification. Often, accounting rules permit companies to choose among two or more alternatives. Chapter 5, in particular, provides examples where companies can make decisions that affect when expenses are included in the income statement. Companies are not required or even encouraged to choose the most conservative accounting convention among permissible alternatives.

However, when companies face an uncertain situation that arises as a company follows a particular accounting convention, conservatism argues for the alternative that results in lower income or lower value for the assets. For example, suppose a company was trying to decide whether to recognize a sale or to wait to recognize the revenue. If the decision is not clear, conservatism probably would argue for postponing recognition.

Conservatism does not require a company to understate income or assets. To intentionally understate income or assets would not be useful to readers of the financial statement. In addition, if companies were permitted to intentionally understate accounting results, managers would be permitted and possibly even encouraged to manipulate accounting results.

DOUBLE-ENTRY

Modern accounting is often described as double-entry. Once a company commits to entering business transactions into an accounting ledger, the company will include all the journal entries only if they include two equal sets of entries for each transaction. For example, if a company uses cash to buy manufacturing equipment, the accounting records are complete only if the company includes the reduction in cash held by the company and also lists the new asset in its records.

The double-entry system is tied to a pattern of entering trades as debits and credits (see Chapter 1). The double-entry system requires that the debits entered into the accounting system match the credits entered into the accounting system.

The double-entry system provides a cross-check that may prevent some mistakes in accounting records. For example, if an incorrect amount is debited or credited, the difference will help detect the error. The double-entry system can help to make sure offsetting transactions are not accidentally omitted from the accounting records.

FULL DISCLOSURE

Accounting records are collected to track the financial results of a company. To be useful to users, both within the company and outside the company, financial statements must present relevant information. Much of that information is contained in the balance sheet, income statement, and statement of cash position. Other relevant information appears in additional schedules and tables included with the financial statements. Additional relevant information appears in footnotes and in discussion published with the statements.

Generally accepted accounting standards dictate much of the disclosure required in financial statements. In addition to specific rules, companies should explain the results adequately to ensure that the disclosures are not misleading.

FOCUS ON ADDITION

One uncommon trait of modern accounting is a focus on addition. If you tell an accountant you bought more of an asset, he or she will record the information on the debit side of a ledger. If you later sell some of the asset, your accountant will record that information as an addition to the numbers on the credit side of the ledger. At the end of the accounting period, the accountant will add up all the debits and separately add up the credits. Only at this point (and only in actually preparing accounting statements) the accountant will net the sum of the debits against the sum of the credits.

Parents of young children may recall when their children came to understand addition. In the early stages, children don't understand subtraction, multiplication, or division. It is tempting to think of accounting as a primitive mathematical system because it relies so heavily on addition.

It is helpful to think back to the explanations of primitive counting systems we described in Chapter 1. When working with urns containing pebbles, it is easy to add or remove (i.e., subtract) pebbles. But tally marks on a clay tablet are hard to remove. Further, once accounting results were recorded on paper ledgers, the system permitted less skilled bookkeepers to record business transactions and did not place high demands on their math skills.

Modern accounting uses computers to handle the math, but the data entry still resembles the pattern resembling a bookkeeper working on paper ledgers.

GENERALLY ACCEPTED ACCOUNTING PRINCIPLES (GAAP)

Most companies must publish annual audited financial statements. Registered public companies and even many private investment companies are required to publish audited statements. Most investors require similar disclosure.

These financial statements generally must conform to the rules set by the FASB. The SEC generally defers to industry rule-making bodies but nevertheless imposes additional requirements. The AICPA also promulgates rules defining acceptable disclosure.

These rules, along with custom and practice, define generally accepted accounting principles. Auditors check statements prior to publication and certify compliance with GAAP.

Outside of the United States, the most widely recognized standard for accounting procedures is the International Financial Reporting Standards (IFRS) promulgated by the International Accounting Standards Board (IASB). Global accounting standards have become more consistent in recent years.

GOING-CONCERN VALUE

Companies often invest in plant and equipment to produce manufacturing equipment and facilities that are worth very little to other economic players. In general, accountants value these assets using going-concern value. Going-concern value reflects the value of assets as they are being used by the present owner. Going-concern value usually equals historical cost rather than the value that could be realized by selling the assets and liquidating the company.

JOURNAL ENTRY

A journal entry is the set of information needed to document a business transaction. The minimum information required for a complete journal entry is the date this journal entry hits the accounting records, the account that will be affected by the entry, whether it is a debit or a credit, and the value of the entry.

Accounting systems generally begin as database management programs. As a result, many additional facts are usually stored along with the minimum data. For example, the posting date records the time and date that the entry entered the database. The data record may include both an account name and account number. The record may include information about the currency used in the business transaction posted as well as additional audit information, such as the source of the information, especially for automated entries.

In addition, while the accounting entry is being created, other records may be established. For example, if a company buys an asset that should be depreciated, information needed to calculate depreciation at a later date may be recorded when the asset enters the accounting records. When investments are entered, information about future interest payments and maturities may enter schedules and records outside the accounting system.

MATCHING

Revenues are recognized according to a variety of accrual rules. These rules are generally intended to make reported earnings more useful to readers of financial statements. Expenses are recognized to match the time when associated revenues are recognized.

MATERIALITY

Despite a variety of rules, accountants do not necessarily need to worry about accounting records that are inaccurate or records that do not comply with GAAP. The standard of materiality means that errors that would not influence users of statements are nevertheless acceptable. The standard of materiality is not a precise mathematical threshold. Errors of a particular dollar amount or percentage may be material in one context and not in another. In addition, if the impact over time or including a series of transactions is material, then the individual entries are probably material.

The standard of materiality may help determine whether a company needs to correct errors or restate prior results under different accounting procedures. The standard of materiality may also help determine whether an approximation or estimate may be used when precise counting is difficult or expensive.

RECOGNITION

Revenue is recognized when it is "earned." This usually occurs when the sale of a good or service is performed. Sale is usually recognized when all or substantially all the work has been completed and there is a reasonable chance of payment.

Some businesses follow specific patterns. Companies that work on long contracts may recognize revenue over the life of the contract. For example, the percentage-of-completion method allocates total revenue based on an assessment of how much of the contract has been accomplished. Companies may recognize this revenue before or after cash payments are made by the customer.

A second pattern used by customers to recognize revenue is the installment method. A company may contract to receive several equal or unequal payments over the life of the contract. The installment method recognizes the revenue as the cash is received.

Note that the installment method applies the cash basis of recognition to a particular contract or transaction. Companies that use the installment method may still use accrual accounting methods for other types of accounting transactions.

Accountants should not recognize revenue unless there is a reasonable chance of payment. In addition, companies generally should not recognize revenue before the service is performed. Companies that have recognized income too early have had to restate earnings. In some instances, companies have faced civil and criminal penalties for recognizing revenue improperly.

UNDERSTANDABILITY

Accounting records are understandable if they follow GAAP, contain adequate disclosures, and apply consistent methods from one year to the next.

USEFULNESS

Accounting records should be both relevant and reliable. To be relevant, account records should be timely and should contain adequate disclosures. To be reliable, accounting records should be accurate, should conform to GAAP, and should be consistent.

VALUATION

In general, accounting financial statements rely on actual or historical cost to determine value for most accounting transactions. The actual transaction amount is verifiable and often occurs as an arm's-length transaction. Once a record enters the accounting system at cost, accountants continue to rely on that cost.

Inventories are generally carried on the balance sheet at the lower of cost or market. For companies that turn over inventory frequently, the cost and market price for inventory may not diverge much, especially if the company removes older inventory costs ahead of recently acquired inventory (FIFO). Also, in periods of generally rising prices, market price will generally be higher than cost.

Accounting rules require holders of financial assets to disclose the fair market value of many of those financial assets. In some cases, the financial statements need to include a footnote with the updated fair value. In other cases, the impact of the change in value may enter the income and balance sheet.

VERIFIABILITY

Users of financial statements need confidence that financial statements are truthful. Companies employ internal auditors who should be responsible for assuring the accuracy and fairness of financial statements. Many financial statements are audited by independent CPAs. In order for internal and independent auditors to be able to determine the accuracy and fairness of financial statements, the company must adopt accounting methods that create evidence that transactions were handled fairly, that the financial statements reflect actual transactions, and that the financial statements reflect all transactions.

CONCLUSION

Many accounting conventions are prescribed by law, regulators, or GAAP. Companies must prepare financial statements consistent with many of the conventions described in this chapter. Users of financial statements must also keep in mind the impact that these conventions have on reported financial results.

Students of accounting should not conclude from this chapter that there is a single right way to account for business transactions. Companies have considerable discretion in the way they account for and report business transactions. GAAP may create considerable latitude for companies to influence the reported results based on how companies decide to handle key accounting conventions. The guidelines in this chapter serve to instruct accountants how to account for business transactions to be useful to readers of financial statements.

2.1. By the end of the first quarter, March 31, 20X1, LCI has no sales or even any saleable inventory. Shares of similar publicly traded technology companies sell for less than book value. Should LCI write down their equity on indications that it is worth less than $5 per share?

2.2. Suppose LCI pays $10 per unit to suppliers to buy 5,000 units of inventory on 6/19/20X1 and sells 3,500 units at $26 on 6/22/20X1. Has the company violated the matching principle because the dollar amount of the sales ($26 × 3,500 = $91,000) and the costs ($10 × 5,000 = $50,000) do not match, the dates of the entries do not match, and the number of units does not match?

CHAPTER 3

Balance Sheet

Chapter 1 presented several accounts that appear on the balance sheet along with how accountants link these accounts together in a highly systematic and structured way. While the chapter discussed only balance sheet accounts, the chapter primarily described the double-entry system. Chapter 2 reviewed some of the conventions accountants use to describe business transactions.

This chapter will show how the double-entry system and the conventions described in Chapter 2 are used to create the balance sheet, one of three key statements described in this text (along with the income statement and the statement of cash flows).

BALANCE SHEET CONTAINS PERMANENT ACCOUNTS

In Chapter 1, we introduced permanent accounts and temporary accounts. Temporary accounts include revenues and expenses. All the remaining accounts, including assets, liabilities, and equity, are reported on the balance sheet (also called the statement of financial position).

The chapter begins by explaining how transactions included on the balance sheet differ from other types of transactions. The chapter also shows how the time horizon of the balance sheet affects which transactions to include. The bulk of the chapter describes the most commonly observed assets, liabilities, and equity that businesses use and how accountants handle them.

TIME LINE OF CASH FLOWS

A balance sheet reflects all journal entries affecting the company since inception. Figure 3.1 contains a time line representing all journal transactions

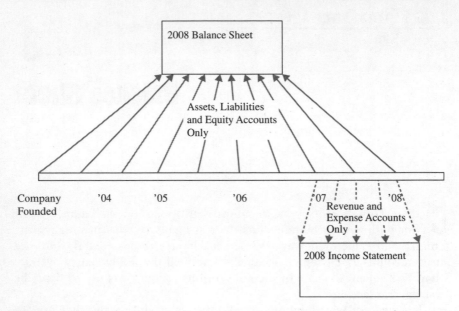

FIGURE 3.1   Time Line of Journaled Transactions

since a company was founded. This particular illustration shows a company that was founded in 2004 and is preparing a balance sheet and income statement at the end of 2008. Notice how all entries that are assembled into the balance sheet are cumulative. That is, they reflect all debits and credits to these accounts for the entire life of the company. These are the accounts that are called permanent accounts.

Historical records indicate that businesses have been in continued existence for hundreds of years in Europe and Asia. It is possible to find businesses in the United States founded before the American Revolution. Had these businesses used modern accounting methods, their balance sheet would include the sum of transactions for that extended period. Indeed, the CASH account on the balance sheet of Ford Motor Company presumably includes the first dollar that Henry Ford ever received from a customer.

The income statement in Figure 3.1 includes only information about transactions that occur in the year 2008. At the beginning of the year, all revenue and expense accounts have balances equal to zero and at the end of the year, these accounts reflect the revenues and expenses for the year. These accounts on the income statement are called temporary accounts and will be discussed in Chapters 4 and 5.

TYPES OF BALANCE SHEET ACCOUNTS

A balance sheet includes three broad types of accounting transactions. This statement includes a cumulative total of all transactions that affect individual asset, liability, and equity accounts. Accountants keep track of individual assets, liabilities, and equities. For example, accountants keep track of cash in one account and inventory in one or more additional asset accounts. Then, the individual accounts are organized and presented on the balance sheet by type.

The three types of balance sheet accounts are described in Chapter 3.

Assets

In Chapter 1, assets were described as company resources that can be valuable to the company either directly or indirectly. Many of these assets are familiar: CASH, ACCOUNTS RECEIVABLE, INVENTORY, INVESTMENTS, BUILDINGS, and LAND.

Companies may own a number of assets that may be difficult to see or touch. Financial assets such as Treasury bills, notes, and bonds may exist as records in a database, although the existence and description of these assets is memorialized in sometimes lengthy documentation.

A number of assets are even less physically tangible. In some cases, legal records document the existence and nature of these assets. Examples include patents, leases, and derivative securities. Other intangibles such as GOODWILL are created by accountants to describe certain business transactions. These assets may not be memorialized in legal documents, board minutes, or business communication.

Another type of asset is created by accountants to affect the timing of revenues and expenses. These accrual entries are described in Chapter 5. Examples of assets created by accountants to handle accrual accounting include PREPAID RENT and ALLOWANCE FOR UNCOLLECTIBLES. A brief description of some of these assets appears later in this chapter.

A final type of asset is called a contra asset. As described in Chapter 1, accountants record an increase in an asset by debiting the asset account and record a decrease by crediting an asset account. Contra accounts reverse the debits and credits—credit to increase a contra asset, and debit to reduce a contra asset. Contra assets are used to report the decline in value of another asset on the balance sheet. See ACCUMULATED DEPRECIATION for an example of a contra asset.

Current Assets   Current assets include all assets that could be expected to be available as cash or can reasonably be expected to convert to cash within a year. The one-year horizon that separates current assets from long-term assets is arbitrary and probably reflects the pattern of reporting financial results annually. A list of current assets companies often own follows.

Cash   Accountants use the word *cash* to include coins, paper money, and bank accounts that do not contain major restrictions on withdrawing the money. CASH includes most deposit accounts that are subject to few holding requirements and little or no market risk if the deposit is exchanged for cash. Still, U.S. law and generally accepted accounting principles (GAAP) classify some deposit-like accounts as INVESTMENTS rather than CASH.

Investments or Short-Term Investments   This account and similarly named accounts contain investments that mature (i.e., they repay principal) within a year of the date that the balance sheet is dated. This account could include U.S. Treasury bills and notes that mature within a year, commercial paper, and bank certificates of deposits maturing within a year. The SHORT-TERM INVESTMENTS account also includes investments that once had a maturity date more than a year after the balance sheet date but have less than one year left until maturity.

GAAP require companies to categorize investments. Some of the investments are carried at cost. Other investments are revalued on the date the balance sheet is published. Short-term investments generally are not very sensitive to changes in interest rates. These investments may, however, contain some risk of default.

Accounts Receivable   This account includes a total of money due from customers. ACCOUNTS RECEIVABLE generally is created when a customer buys a good or service and doesn't pay immediately. ACCOUNTS RECEIVABLE may earn interest, often after a grace period immediately following a sale. Companies have differing success in collecting interest on unpaid balances.

Most customers pay for goods and services within a month or two, so companies are generally permitted to carry the value as a current asset. In fact, if a company makes a sale to a customer expecting to receive payment over a longer period, the unpaid amount will usually be formalized with a note or other document more completely describing the lending terms being offered by the manufacturer. Those longer-term trade credits are not included in ACCOUNTS RECEIVABLE until the company expects to be paid within a year.

Companies can "factor" their accounts receivable. The company transfers the asset to someone who will wait for repayment. The financing company, in return, provides cash to the company that created the accounts receivable. Because a company can usually quickly convert accounts receivables into cash, accountants are comfortable classifying these accounts as current assets.

Companies recognize that some of the money owed will be uncollectible. Companies estimate the uncollectible amount in an account called ALLOWANCE FOR UNCOLLECTIBLES. The ACCOUNTS RECEIVABLE published on the balance sheet reduces the total amount due by the amount in the allowance account. Chapter 5 describes how the allowance account functions in greater detail.

Inventory Inventory is an asset because it has value that the company expects to convert to cash at some point. Inventory is a current asset because the company usually converts the goods into cash within a year.

Inventory may be items purchased or items manufactured. The inventory may include items available for sale as well as raw materials that are required by a manufacturer. In all cases, inventory is recognized as an asset. Companies spend cash to acquire these goods, but the company does not recognize this cash outflow as expense. Instead, one asset, cash, is exchanged for another item or items carried in the inventory account.

Manufacturers usually carry inventory in three separate accounts. RAW MATERIALS inventory reflects the cost to acquire inputs to the manufacturing process. WORK IN PROCESS inventory includes the cost of goods not yet completed. FINISHED GOODS inventory includes the cost of goods ready for sale.

Many cash payments that are commonly called expenses in everyday English actually are included in the inventory account. For example, the FINISHED GOODS account contains the cost of labor used to convert RAW MATERIALS into FINISHED GOODS. In fact, one of the goals of cost accounting is to associate costs to an inventory account whenever possible.

The inventory accounts at a manufacturer accumulate costs from different stages of the manufacturing process over time. The inventory accounts at a retailing firm hold the costs to acquire merchandise available for sale. In both cases, the inventory account affects when these costs enter the income statement. Chapter 5 will deal in detail with the issue of timing.

When goods are sold, the costs that are being carried in the inventory accounts enter the income statement. Chapter 4 describes that process. Inventory presents a special problem for accountants when the company has paid different prices for identical inventory. Companies can assume that they are selling the inventory with the oldest costs first (the first-in, first-out or FIFO method), the most recent costs first (the last-in, first-out or LIFO method), or a weighted average cost. Companies are free to choose any of these three methods, but they should be consistent over time.

The LIFO method includes current costs in the income statement so that reported earnings will be most consistent with the profits reflecting prevailing costs. Because older costs remain in the inventory account, the balance sheet may not carry inventory at the current price. FIFO removes the oldest costs so the balance sheet reflects the cost of the most recently acquired inventory, but the income statement may include some inventory gains and losses. The impact of price changes is small for a company that turns over inventory several times a year. If inventory costs generally rise over time, then LIFO will result in lower income than FIFO, so companies can reduce taxable income using LIFO for tax reporting.

Long-Term Assets   Long-term assets are assets that either can't be readily turned into cash or mature more than a year in the future. Examples of long-term assets are below.

Companies carry LAND, IMPROVEMENTS, BUILDINGS, and EQUIPMENT in separate accounts. Differences in the way accountants handle each type of asset are described along with each asset type.

Land   Companies acquire land to create manufacturing space, build stores, or create office space for administrative workers. LAND is generally carried on the balance sheet at historical cost. While buildings, improvements, and equipment wear out, accountants assume that land does not wear out, so they do not include any of the cost of acquiring the land in the income statement.

If land is acquired to build a mine or an oil well, the value of the land does erode as the mineral or oil is extracted. In this case, income statement includes an expense equal to the cost of the land plus any development necessary to extract the resource minus the salvage value. This decline is called depletion. This decrease in value builds up in an ACCUMULATED DEPLETION account.

Accountants calculate the amount of depletion and estimate the total number of units to be extracted. The cost per unit equals the value of the depletion divided by the predicted number of units. Accountants include an expense equal to this cost per unit times the actual units of the natural resource recovered in each accounting period. Chapter 5 discusses how depletion expenses affect the income statement.

Improvements or Land Improvements   IMPROVEMENTS include the costs to build roads, fences, lighting, parking lots, and landscaping. Improvements are generally carried on the balance sheet at historical cost. The value of the improvements erodes due to wear and tear, changing needs, and style. The income statement includes an expense equal to the cost of the improvements minus the salvage value. This decline is called depreciation. This decrease in value builds up in an ACCUMULATED DEPRECIATION account.

Accountants calculate the amount of depreciation and estimate the useful life of the improvements. The cost is allocated over time using either the straight-line method, units-of-activity method, declining-balance method, sum-of-the-years' digits method, or modified accelerated cost recovery system (MACRS). The straight-line method recognizes an equal decline in value each year. The units-of-activity method or production method allocates the decline over units of production. The other methods recognize the decline in value faster in the earlier period and a smaller decline in the later period in which the improvements are expected to provide benefits to the company. Chapter 5 discusses how depreciation expenses affect the income statement.

Buildings The BUILDINGS account holds the costs to build structures used for manufacturing, retailing, and office workers. Buildings are generally carried on the balance sheet at historical cost. The value of the buildings erodes due to wear and tear, changing needs, and style. The income statement includes an expense equal to the cost of the buildings minus the salvage value. This decline is also called depreciation. This decrease in value builds up in an ACCUMULATED DEPRECIATION account. Accountants calculate depreciation on buildings the same way as they do for improvements.

Equipment EQUIPMENT includes tools, manufacturing equipment, and office equipment. Equipment is generally carried on the balance sheet at historical cost. The value of the equipment erodes due to wear and tear, changing needs, and style. The income statement includes an expense equal to the cost of the equipment minus the salvage value. This decline is also called depreciation. This decrease in value also builds up in an ACCUMULATED DEPRECIATION account. Accountants calculate depreciation on equipment the same way as they do for improvements.

Patent A PATENT grants exclusive right to use an idea for many years. The cost of internally obtaining a patent is generally not included on the balance sheet. However, if the company buys a patent from another party, the cost is included initially at the historical cost. The value of this patent erodes due to the passage of time, changing needs, and new technologies. The income statement includes an expense equal to the cost of the patent. This decline is called amortization. Unlike depreciation, this decrease in value reduces the value of the patent in the accounting records and on the balance sheet.

Goodwill   When a company buys another company and pays more than book value, the increment enters the balance sheet as GOODWILL. GOODWILL acknowledges that the excess over book value is real and persistent, reflecting value for managerial skill, the value of assets above their historical cost, and general market conditions. GOODWILL is not amortized. However, companies must assess the value of GOODWILL and lower the value if necessary.

Research-and-Development Costs   Research-and-development costs are not included on the balance sheet. Companies may argue that these costs provide benefits to the company over time. Nevertheless, GAAP do not permit companies to hold costs as an asset on the balance sheet. Instead, these journal entries enter the income statement as the costs are incurred.

Liabilities

The assets of the company are financed by liabilities and equity.

Current Liabilities   Current liabilities are obligations the company expects to pay within one year. Several types of current liabilities are listed below with a brief description of the liability.

Accounts Payable   ACCOUNTS PAYABLE is the unpaid obligations to suppliers. Generally, the obligation to pay is documented only by a sales invoice. No formal lending agreement exists, but the amount due may be subject to interest if payment is delayed.

Notes Payable   When a written document exists defining the terms of a lending agreement, accountants generally record the liability in NOTES PAYABLE, rather than in ACCOUNTS PAYABLE. The note may be due to a bank or other lender, or it could be an agreement with the supplier that is formalized into a note.

Interest Payable   Interest is payable on the maturity of a note or bond and periodically during the life of the note or bond. At the end of an accounting period, many of the notes and bonds have earned interest equal to a portion of the periodic payment. The interest is a legal obligation, but the company would not expect to pay interest for this fractional period until the interest payment date. INTEREST PAYABLE documents the interest already earned on these loan agreements.

Salary Payable Pay periods may not correspond exactly with the dates used to publish financial statements. Companies may owe salary for a fractional pay period. The company may have other similar accounts for employment taxes.

Income Tax Payable Companies file quarterly income tax forms, but most companies make regular corporate income tax payments during the quarter. The INCOME TAX PAYABLE handles the mismatch between the cash payments and the tax obligations.

Advances from Customers Some businesses require advanced payment from customers. Companies that produce customized products may demand partial or complete payment before beginning production. Companies that sell goods that take months or years to manufacture may receive partial payment during the period in which the order is being completed.

Estimated Warranty Liability If a company has substantial expenses for warranty claims, it may recognize that responsibility by creating an ESTIMATED WARRANTY LIABILITY. Companies recognize an estimated warranty expense at the time of sale (a debit) and a credit to this liability. Chapter 5 will discuss the issue of timing of expenses.

Long-Term Liabilities Long-term liabilities are obligations due more than a year in the future. Companies may have several types of long-term liabilities. The most common long-term liabilities are described next.

Bonds Companies issue bonds to raise money to carry on and expand the business. Bonds are formal lending agreements. Investors lend money to the company and receive regular interest and repayment at maturity.

Companies may have many bond issues that they account for separately. Nevertheless, companies generally carry this liability approximately at historical cost. However, if the company issued bonds at a discount, the company must create a schedule to revalue the bonds so that the carrying cost equals the face amount of debt at maturity.

Capital Leases Leases create an obligation to make periodic payments in return for use of equipment or buildings. Operating leases do not appear on the balance sheet because the benefit provided roughly matches the payment. The payments are included on the income statement as they are paid to the lessor.

Capital leases resemble the outright purchase of an asset along with the issuance of debt. If certain conditions are true, a company needs to value the asset and the liability and include both on the balance sheet.

Pensions   Companies do not list pension plan assets or liabilities on the balance sheet. Companies must, however, report the difference on the balance sheet. If plan assets exceed liabilities, that difference is reported as an asset. If plan liabilities exceed plan assets, the difference is reported as a liability.

Equity

The owners of a company own equity in the company. The most common form of ownership is common stock, but accountants accumulate this ownership in a number of accounts, including the par amount of common, the additional amount paid above the par value of the common, and retained earnings. Companies may have more than one class of common stock. Companies may have preferred stock, treasury stock, and other accounts. Partnerships have different categories of ownership. The most common types of equity are listed next.

Common Stock   The value of common stock issued is carried on the balance sheet at historical cost. If the common shares have a par value or stated value, the common stock is included as that par value or stated value times the number of shares issued. If the stock was issued for more than the par or stated value, the excess is recorded in a separate account as additional paid-in capital.

Retained Earnings   At the end of a year, the temporary accounts (revenues and expenses) are used to create the income statement. Then, the values in each of these accounts are set to zero and the net income or loss enters the balance sheet as RETAINED EARNINGS.

Dividends are paid out of RETAINED EARNINGS. As long as the company has enough cash to repay debt and redeem preferred stock, the common shareholders own the RETAINED EARNINGS and it is part of the equity of the firm.

Treasury Stock   Treasury stock is common stock that has been reacquired by the company. It is carried on the balance sheet at historical cost. This account is a contra-equity account. The treasury stock reduces the amount of equity outstanding.

Preferred Stock The value of preferred stock is carried on the balance sheet at historical cost. If the preferred stock has a par value, then the value in the PREFERRED STOCK account is the par amount per share times the number of preferred shares issued. If the preferred stock was issued for more or less than the par value, the difference is carried in an account with a name like ADDITIONAL PAID-IN CAPITAL IN EXCESS OF PAR VALUE—PREFERRED STOCK.

PRESENTING THE CLASSIFIED BALANCE SHEET

Table 3.1 shows a classified balance sheet for Lavaliere Industries.

The balance sheet first shows current assets, followed by long-term assets, current liabilities, long-term liabilities, and equity. In this case, the most recent results are presented as well as results from the previous year, along with a comparison.

TABLE 3.1 Balance Sheet: Lavaliere Industries, December 31, 20X2 ($000)

	20X2	20X1	Difference
ASSETS			
CASH	$133,000	$ 66,000	$67,000
ACCOUNTS RECEIVABLE	70,000	60,000	10,000
MERCHANDISE INVENTORY	30,000	20,000	10,000
PREPAID EXPENSES	5,000	2,000	3,000
LAND	200,000	100,000	100,000
BUILDINGS	320,000	130,000	190,000
ACCUMULATED DEPRECIATION— BLDG	(22,000)	(10,000)	(12,000)
EQUIPMENT	54,000	20,000	34,000
ACCUMULATED DEPRECIATION— EQUIPMENT	(6,000)	(2,000)	(4,000)
TOTAL ASSETS	$784,000	$386,000	
LIABILITIES AND SHAREHOLDERS' EQUITY			
ACCOUNTS PAYABLE	56,000	24,000	32,000
INCOME TAX PAYABLE	12,000	16,000	(4,000)
BONDS PAYABLE	160,000	125,000	35,000
COMMON STOCK	180,000	125,000	55,000
RETAINED EARNINGS	376,000	96,000	280,000
TOTAL LIABILITIES AND SHAREHOLDERS' EQUITY			
	$784,000	$386,000	

CONCLUSION

The balance sheet reports on the value of the assets, liabilities, and equity for the firm. These accounts are called permanent accounts, so the balance sheet reflects all the journal entries that have affected these accounts since the company began recording business transactions in the accounting system.

3.1. Following is a list of all the balance sheet accounts that have been used in the questions in this book. Next to each account is the sum of all the debits to that account and the sum of all credits to that account. Note that these totals reflect all the debits and credits to each account in all chapters of the text, not just the previous two chapters. Use the information to construct a balance sheet for LCI.

Account	Debits	Credits
CASH	$6,490,001	$5,433,450
SECURITY DEPOSITS	4,000	0
ADVANCES TO SUPPLIERS	250,000	250,000
ACCOUNTS RECEIVABLE	932,500	641,000
ALLOWANCE FOR UNCOLLECTIBLES	25,564	59,029
FINISHED GOODS INVENTORY	650,000	645,000
PREPAID RENT	4,000	4,000
INVESTMENT IN BONDS	2,000,000	0
EQUIPMENT	45,000	0
ACCUMULATED DEPRECIATION	0	11,250
PATENTS	2,000,000	200,000
ACCOUNTS PAYABLE	215,450	315,450
PAYROLL TAXES PAYABLE	120,000	120,000
COMMON STOCK	0	1,000,000
PAID-IN CAPITAL IN EXCESS OF PAR	0	$4,000,000

CHAPTER 4

Adding an Income Statement

We have seen that it is possible to process many common business transactions without using an income statement (also called statement of earnings). Generally accepted accounting principles (GAAP) require companies to produce both a balance sheet and an income statement, along with a variety of additional reports, schedules, and footnotes. This chapter will show how the income statement is a major extension to the way we posted transactions such as SALES, INTEREST EXPENSE, and COST OF GOODS SOLD.

In Chapter 1, we introduced a number of accounts (represented as separate urns or clay tablets) to count myrrh, currency, and other assets, a number of liabilities, and equity. These accounts are called permanent accounts because they are not reset at the beginning of each new accounting period. For example, if you were using an urn to count cash, you would begin a new year with the same count of cash with which you ended the year.

Permanent accounts accumulate all the debits and credits that have ever been applied to each account since the beginning of the business. The values accumulated in a centuries-old business include any and all business transactions that have affected each account for those many years.

Management and investors frequently look at how these permanent accounts change over time. For example, a lender may look at cash and money market investments over time to spot trends in the company's ability to handle cash flow needs.

TEMPORARY ACCOUNTS

The company's net worth warrants much attention from preparers and readers of financial statements. The retained earnings of a company contains a total of all the business transactions that affect the wealth of the owners. This is, of course, another permanent account, but accountants have produced another type of account—the temporary account—to track the company's success in building wealth for the owners.

Retained earnings measures the value of the owners' interest that stems from profits and losses. It is possible to track the value of this equity account over time to get an insight on the profitability and financial health of a company. For example, you might note the size of retained earnings at the end of each quarter. That method provides information only as frequently as each reporting period (usually quarterly). And the analysis does not document why the equity of the company rises or falls.

Accountants developed an income statement to document the annual and quarterly changes in company equity. All of these accounts are called temporary accounts because they are reset to zero at the beginning of each fiscal year. Therefore, temporary accounts reflect only business transactions in the current period (generally a quarter or year).

In addition, many different temporary accounts are created to expand the understanding of changes to the equity accounts. In fact, these temporary accounts appear on the income statement, and the balance sheet is made up of permanent accounts.

The results of the income statement are included on the balance sheet as an adjustment to equity. During the year, the income is included as RESULTS OF CURRENT OPERATIONS or a similarly named account. On published year-end statements, the income from the entire year is usually included in an equity account called RETAINED EARNINGS. Because income is included as equity, the balance sheet will match the balance sheet produced by the simplified accounting methods described in Chapter 1.

Figure 4.1 reproduces the time line in Figure 3.1 that represents the timing of all accounting transactions since a business was formed. As can be seen from the figure, the permanent accounts on the balance sheet include all debits and credits to permanent accounts since inception. Temporary accounts include only the entries to income statement accounts during a single accounting period (e.g., one year).

As indicated in Chapter 1, revenues and expenses reflect increases in the equity of the company. The impact of 2008 income is included on the balance sheet as an equity account called RETAINED EARNINGS. RETAINED EARNINGS would include the net income for 2004 through 2007 as well.

USING TEMPORARY ACCOUNTS

Temporary accounts include revenue accounts and expense accounts. Revenues include SALES and INTEREST INCOME. Expenses include

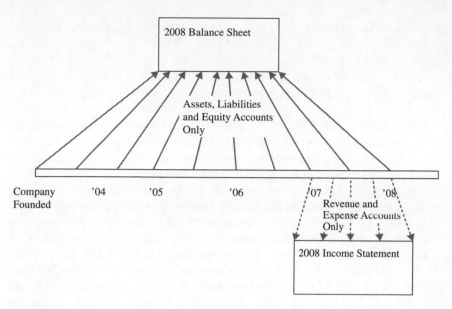

FIGURE 4.1 Time Line of Journaled Transactions

COST OF GOODS SOLD, INTEREST EXPENSE, PAYROLL, and RENT.

Using the methods in Chapter 1, it is easy to see the sale of a good delivered from inventory as an exchange of the item in inventory for currency. In Chapter 1, we saw the reduction of the asset (INVENTORY) roughly offset the increase in the asset (CASH). As explained earlier, accountants would generally remove the inventory at cost and post the actual cash received. The net difference would represent an increase in net worth (i.e., an equity account).

For example, if we sold an item that cost $50 for a retail price of $80, we could, using the primitive accounting in Chapter 1, simply remove the asset from our books (using cost), reflect the inflow of cash for the sale, and account for the difference as an increase in net worth:

Account	Debit	Credit
CASH	$80	
INVENTORY		$50
EQUITY		$30

In fact, accountants follow a much more complicated procedure:

Account	Debit	Credit
CASH	$80	
SALES		$80
COST OF GOODS SOLD	$50	
INVENTORY		$50

The SALES and COST OF GOODS SOLD accounts are temporary accounts, and the CASH and INVENTORY accounts are permanent accounts. The temporary accounts get reset to zero at the end of each accounting period. Later, these temporary accounts will be merged into equity.

In the first method, net worth or equity grows by the net profit on the trade or $30. In the second example, the entire value of the cash received is counted as an increase in equity (in the form of the temporary account SALES). Likewise, the entire amount of the reduction in inventory is counted as a loss in equity. While the $80 increase and the $50 decrease net to the same $30 profit, this income statement preserves the individual contributions toward that profit. In summary, the credit of $80 to SALES and the debit of $50 to COST OF GOODS SOLD will eventually become a credit and debit to EQUITY (specifically, RETAINED EARNINGS).

It is tempting to say that the modern method exaggerates the impact of individual transactions on firm equity by failing to acknowledge that the $80 revenue is possible only when it accompanies a transfer of $50 in inventory to the customer. In fact, the modern income statement goes a step further in separating the components. Instead of including only the markup on the trade of $30, the entire sale is booked as if it represented an increase in equity of $80. The amount is temporarily (i.e., for the rest of the accounting period) held in the temporary account SALES, but this temporary account represents an increase in net worth by the same amount. The reduction of inventory shows up without offset as a reduction in net worth (through the use of a temporary account called COST OF GOODS SOLD).

Finally, these gross (not net) impacts on net worth are carried around for the rest of the accounting period, or to the end of the fiscal year. The gross amount of sales accumulates, as does the cost of goods sold, along with a variety of temporary accounts. These temporary accounts provide a wealth of information.

TYPES OF TRANSACTIONS INVOLVING TEMPORARY ACCOUNTS

Entries to temporary accounts are frequently paired with entries to permanent accounts. For example, revenues are matched to assets in the examples below:

Account	Debit	Credit
CASH	$80	
SALES		$80

The preceding transaction reflects the actual receipt of cash (a permanent account). At least with this pair of entries, the company wealth increases by an amount temporarily subtotaled in the category SALES.

Notice, too, that the preceding transactions do not pair the temporary account SALES with an offsetting COST OF GOODS SOLD, another temporary account. Under most cases, the two are not equal, unless the sale is made at break-even levels. Likewise, the impact on the balance sheet is generally not equal. A decrease in the asset account INVENTORY is less than the increase in the CASH account. The net profit is carried in the temporary accounts until the end of the fiscal year.

In the following set of transactions, $100 of interest income, a temporary account, is received as cash, a permanent account. The increase in net worth is temporarily held in the revenue account INTEREST INCOME. Later in the accounting year, the balance in the INTEREST INCOME account would be closed out and replaced by an increase in a balance sheet such as RETAINED EARNINGS.

Account	Debit	Credit
CASH	$100	
INTEREST INCOME		$100

Note that accountants may not wait for the actual receipt of cash to recognize some of the income. Suppose the total interest payment will be $100, reflecting interest of $50 earned in each of two accounting periods. In the following example, half of the interest is recorded in the current statement period and half will be recorded in the next month (not shown here).

Account	Debit	Credit
ACCRUED INTEREST	$50	
INTEREST INCOME		$50

In this example, INTEREST INCOME recognizes income that has not yet been received. Because the word *interest* appears in both account names, it is important to distinguish the asset (ACCRUED INTEREST) from the revenue account (INTEREST INCOME). Here, the temporary account (and ultimately the equity account, too) recognizes this income somewhat independently of the actual flow of cash. This recognition of accounting entries is somewhat independent of the timing of the receipt of cash. This is an example of accrual accounting and will be discussed in greater detail in the next chapter.

Frequently, expense accounts are paired with balance sheet accounts, too.

Account	Debit	Credit
INTEREST EXPENSE	$100	
CASH		$100

In this transaction, cash is used to pay owners of company bonds. As with the preceding example, where interest income matches the actual payments made, it is also possible for the company to book income whether or not cash has been received:

Account	Debit	Credit
INTEREST EXPENSE	$50	
INTEREST PAYABLE		$50

Here, the company recognizes that it owes money before the money is payable to investors. In this example, $50 of the interest expense for the loan for the two-month period enters the company accounts after one month and affects the profitability of the company before the payment occurs. The expense is recognized by the company before the amount must be paid.

INCOME ACCOUNTS

Accountants have, of course, adopted the income statement and all the temporary accounts on the income statement. A list of common income statement items appears below. This list is not complete, however. Chapter 5 introduces additional revenue and expense accounts and the concept of accrual accounting.

Revenues

Sales   The SALES account reflects the price times the quantity of a purchase by a customer. SALES may be reported as NET SALES where returns and discounts significantly impact sales.

Service Revenue   Service companies may classify sales revenue as SERVICE REVENUE to emphasize that the customers are not buying merchandise.

Interest Income   INTEREST INCOME is nonoperating income for most businesses. This revenue is not included in gross revenue or operating revenue.

Gain on Sale of Equipment   Gains are nonrecurring items. They are not included in gross profit or operating profit.

Expenses

Cost of Goods Sold   The COST OF GOODS SOLD is the largest expense for many companies. When a company sells merchandise from inventory, the assets of the firm decline by the historical cost of the inventory (a credit). The matching debit is the COST OF GOODS SOLD expense account.

By holding costs in an account called INVENTORY, the company postpones entering these costs on the income statement. When the merchandise is sold, the cost is transferred from the balance sheet as inventory onto the income statement as COST OF GOODS SOLD.

Salaries   When salaries appear on the income statement, they are not associated with manufacturing. Wages and salaries of workers creating merchandise are held in inventory accounts until the goods are sold. The cost of employee wages and salaries involved in manufacturing enter the income statement as COST OF GOODS SOLD.

Administrative Expenses   ADMINISTRATIVE EXPENSES may include a large number and different kinds of costs, including salaries, office supplies, postage, and telephone charges for people involved in support functions, not involved in manufacture or delivery of services. Administrative costs are operating expenses.

Selling Expenses   SELLING EXPENSES are operating expenses associated with the sale or marketing of the company's products.

Rent   If rent appears on an income statement, it is probably an operating expense. Although it is possible to rent manufacturing facilities, that cost should be included in the cost of INVENTORY and eventually in the COST OF GOODS SOLD.

Interest Expense   Interest expense is an operating expense. Although the interest may be attributable to bonds issued to build manufacturing facilities, the use of debt is a financing decision, and this cost will not be included in COST OF GOODS SOLD.

Loss on Sale of Discontinued Operations   Losses have the same impact on equity as expenses. This loss is a nonrecurring item that would not be included when calculating operating income.

SINGLE-STEP INCOME STATEMENT

The single-step income statement is organized like the income statement in Table 4.1. The single-step income statement lists all revenues, then all expenses, followed by net income:

MULTISTEP INCOME STATEMENT

The multistep income statement subtracts COST OF GOODS SOLD from SALES to get gross profit. Then, operating expenses are subtracted from gross profit to display operating profit. Finally, nonoperating and nonrecurring revenues and expenses are netted from operating profit to get net income (see Table 4.2).

TABLE 4.1   Income Statement: Lavaliere Industries for the Year Ending 20X2 ($000)

Revenues		
NET SALES	$1,014,000	
INTEREST INCOME	$ 24,000	
Total Revenues		1,038,000
Expenses		
COST OF GOODS SOLD	300,000	
OPERATING EXPENSES (includes $18,000 DEPRECIATION)	240,000	
INTEREST EXPENSE	84,000	
INCOME TAX EXPENSE	94,000	
LOSS ON SALE OF EQUIPMENT	6,000	
Total Expenses		724,000
Net Income		$314,000

TABLE 4.2 Income Statement: Dayton Drilling Co. for the Year Ending 20X2

Sales Revenues		
SALES	$425,000	
SALES RETURNS	21,250	
SALES DISCOUNTS	42,500	
NET SALES		361,250
COST OF GOODS SOLD	234,318	
Gross Profit		126,438
Operating Expenses		
SELLING EXPENSE	5,419	
ADMINISTRATIVE EXPENSE	9,031	
Total Operating Expenses		14,450
Operating Income		111,988
Other Revenues and Gains		
INTEREST INCOME	2,800	
Gain on Sale of Equipment	1,500	9,700
Other Expenses and Losses		
INTEREST EXPENSE	2,800	
CASUALTY LOSS	822	3,622
Net Income		$118,066

CONCLUSION

The income statement contains only items that can affect the retained earnings (revenues, expenses, gains, and losses). Accountants start each financial period with no accumulated results in any of these income accounts so that the income statement reflects the results for that fiscal period only. In contrast, the balance sheet reflects all business transactions since inception that affect those balance sheet accounts.

Users of the income statement look for results for a particular period. The income statement can provide valuable insights into the factors that contribute to the financial success of a company during that period.

4.1. Rent payments are due on the first day of each month beginning March 1. Show entries through year-end.

4.2. You decide to lease additional patents from the company. On March 31, you make the first quarterly payment of $30,000 to license additional patents from Lavalier Bermuda PLC.

4.3. You ship 3,500 NCDs on June 22 to OEM Communications for a gross price of $26 per unit to be paid within 30 days.

4.4. On June 30, you receive semiannual interest on the bond. You leave the June 30 payment in your bank account.

4.5. You receive payment in full on July 18 for the June sales to OEM Communications.

4.6. Oops. It is early January 20X2. Although LCI received monthly statements from the bank, they haven't booked the interest income totaling $31,125.66 for 20X1. LCI accountants discuss the matter with LCI's auditor, who suggests they enter the total in one entry on 12/31/20X1 since LCI has not closed the books yet.

4.7. Following is a list of all the income statement accounts that have been used in the questions in this book. Next to each account is the sum of all the debits to that account and the sum of all credits to that account. Note that these totals reflect all the debits and credits to each account in all chapters of the text, not just the previous three chapters.

Use the information to construct an income statement for LCI.

Account	Debits	Credits
SALES REVENUE	$ 0	$1,697,125
INTEREST REVENUE	0	131,126
COST OF GOODS SOLD	645,000	0
SALARY EXPENSE	480,000	0
COMMISSION EXPENSE	70,450	0
PAYROLL TAX EXPENSE	120,000	0
RENT EXPENSE	44,000	0
UNCOLLECTIBLE ACCOUNT EXPENSE	80,215	0
DEPRECIATION EXPENSE—EQUIPMENT	11,250	0
AMORTIZATION EXPENSE—PATENTS	200,000	0
PATENT LICENSE EXPENSE	$120,000	$ 0

CHAPTER 5

Timing and Accrual Accounting

We have now created the two major accounting statements—the balance sheet and the income statement. We need to introduce accrual accounting before all the basic foundations of financial accounting are in place.

JOURNALING ACCOUNTING TRANSACTIONS

Chapter 1 used T-accounts to describe a small number of myrrh transactions in a small street market. Chapter 4 used a journal of debits and credits to introduce the income statement. The journal imitates earlier paper accounting systems and provides an organized way to input data to computer-based accounting systems. Chapter 5 relies on lists of journals because they concisely describe how accountants view business transactions. They document which accounts are affected by the business transactions, the size of the transactions, and when the transactions occur.

To the student who is comfortable with double-entry accounting but not familiar with how it is used to account for modern business transactions, journal entries help to describe how accountants view business transactions. In the examples that follow, pay attention to what account or accounts contain the debit entry and what account or accounts contain the credit entry.

CASH BASIS ACCOUNTING

Up to now, we have presented cash basis accounting, although we did not identify it as such. Cash basis accounting uses the timing of the receipt of cash to determine when accounting expenses and income are included in the financial records.

Individuals file their tax returns using cash basis accounting. Few of us bother to create double-entry transactions, but we could do so. The IRS doesn't care much about the assets and liabilities. The only entries we need to include in our tax reporting are income and expenses. But our reports to the IRS are the same as if we did create a general ledger system, and we really don't have to post all of these trades. We need to keep track of a few facts about our stock investments and other assets, but they really concern the IRS only if we sell them and generate gains or losses.

Individuals and companies on the cash basis report revenues (salary, interest income, book royalties) and expenses (state income taxes, property taxes, interest expenses on a house) when the cash is paid or received. If you pay a little bit more state income tax in December, you include that expense (although the IRS instead calls it a deduction) in the tax form for that year. Postpone a bonus until January, and that income gets included in the tax year it is paid.

Some businesses can use cash basis accounting (along with double-entry bookkeeping). Sole proprietorships include their income on the individual tax forms of the owners. Not surprisingly, those businesses follow the same basis as the individual owner.

Cash basis accounting has a verifiable standard that determines when revenues and expenses must be included in the income statement. Accountants understand that some of these revenues and expenses may be known to the company or at least could be accurately anticipated. However, the precise point when these income accounts enter the income statement is called the point of recognition.

As objective as cash basis accounting is, the method is subject to manipulation. Companies can and do time cash flows for the benefit of individual taxpayers. While the IRS permits a bit of latitude on individual tax returns, they do not grant much flexibility.

ACCRUAL BASIS ACCOUNTING

A business organized as a C corporation is not permitted to use cash basis accounting. Instead, these companies must use accrual accounting. Accrual accounting includes income and expenses in the income statement in an organized and systematic way to try to get a more accurate view on the timing and size of revenues and expenses.

Accountants will recognize and incorporate revenues and expenses based on a number of rules described in this chapter.

Speed Up Recognizing Expenses

The accounts payable department of any company receives piles of bills for goods and services already provided to a company. If the company is on the cash basis, expenses that are paid 60 or 90 days later would enter the accounting records only when the cash is paid. This delay means that the expense may be recognized well after the benefits have been realized.

To better match the timing of the expense to the benefit derived from the service, accrual accounting will post the expense when the benefit is realized.

For example, if a company hires outside contractors to provide manufacturing or administrative support, and if the contractor invoices the company in the middle of the following month, an accountant might create the following entries to recognize the expense before the contractor is paid:

12/31/X1	PROFESSIONAL EXPENSE	$10,000	
	ACCOUNTS PAYABLE		$10,000

Later, the company receives an invoice and pays it:

1/18/X2	ACCOUNTS PAYABLE	$10,000	
	CASH		$10,000

Notice that, in this case, the company recognizes the expense in the month the service was provided, even though the contractor receives the money in the next calendar year.

When a company using accrual accounting receives a service or good that should be recognized as an expense, the company should recognize the expense when the benefit is realized. It may be difficult to identify a precise date when the expense should be realized. In fact, it may be impossible to identify a single day when the benefits are enjoyed. Accountants make reasonable decisions, and the statements reflect many such choices. The statements will be useful if the company takes reasonable care to recognize the expenses reasonably.

Few companies are tempted to recognize expenses early. However, there are cases, following a reorganization or in a period when the company is expecting to report poor accounting results anyway, a company may be tempted to frontload or otherwise overstate expenses. These companies may think that a larger loss may not matter much to investors, and front-loading expenses sets the stage for a recovery in net income. Companies have been found guilty of arbitrarily accelerating expenses to manipulate future results. Following is a list of some accrued expenses:

Accrued Expenses

SALARY

INTEREST EXPENSE

DEPRECIATION

DEPLETION

AMORTIZATION

WARRANTY EXPENSE

Speed Up Recognizing Income

Most business managers would like to recognize revenue as soon as possible. When a business provides a service to a customer, it is customary to recognize the revenue before the customer has paid the cash for the service. As long as the business is on the accrual basis, the accountants are willing to recognize the revenue as soon as the service has been provided if there is a reasonably good chance that the revenue will be collected from the customer.

The following transactions recognize income for a service provided a month before the customer pays for the service:

1/14/X2	PROFESSIONAL SERVICE INCOME	$12,000	
	ACCOUNTS RECEIVABLE		$12,000
2/13/X2	ACCOUNTS RECEIVABLE	$12,000	
	CASH		$12,000

Managers of companies are frequently compensated based on accounting results. These managers may benefit from compensation plans that exceed certain financial milestones. Following is a list of some accrued revenues, or revenues on contract using percentage completion:

Accrued Revenues

INTEREST INCOME

SUBSCRIPTION REVENUE

Delay Recognizing Income

Some businesses demand payment at the point a transaction is made, with the actual delivery of goods occurring later. Suppose, for example, that a company wants to shift production of a product to a contract manufacturer. A contract manufacturer may accept a contract only if the customer makes a substantial prepayment in advance. The contract manufacturer uses the payment to buy materials and pay other expenses during the production processes. Still, the manufacturer may delay recognizing the income until the goods are finished and shipped to the customer:

1/15/X2	CASH	$100,000	
	UNEARNED SALES REVENUE		$100,000

This pair of transactions reflects the payment of cash on the books of the contract manufacturer. The offsetting transaction is not SALES because the company has not yet manufactured the goods. The liability account UN-EARNED SALES REVENUE reflects the deposit made at the start of the manufacturing period. Following is a list of deferred income:

Deferred Income

Prepaid phone revenue

Subscriptions

Professional retainers

Access to pipeline

Legal retainers

Broadband capacity

In each case, a company has been paid for benefits it has not provided. Holding the amount equal to the cash payment as a liability allows the company to postpone recognizing revenue before the company has earned the revenue.

Delay Recognizing Expenses

When we created balance sheets early in the text, we made an effort to include all business transaction directly on the balance sheet. Any outflow of cash was either a purchase of an asset, which had no effect on the net worth of the company, or something we later called expenses, which lowers the equity of the company. In addition, there are a variety of transactions that are a bit less clear. These are examples of deferred expenses, and two are listed here:

Deferred Expenses

Inventories

Investment in equipment

Accountants so universally use inventory to match the timing of costs to revenues that it is easy to forget that the technique postpones recognition of expenses. In fact, a company may be able to hold costs in inventory accounts even if the company is on a cash basis instead of accrual.

When a company buys equipment that will be used for many years, it does not recognize the purchase price as an expense. Instead, accrual accounting posts the equipment as an asset at the purchase price. Then, over time, accountants create other entries to reflect the wear and tear over the useful life of the equipment. These types of accrual transactions will be described later in this chapter.

Prepaid Expenses

Companies may pay for services in advance for a number of reasons. It is common to pay subscriptions for a year or more in advance. Rental agreements may require the renter to pay one or more months of rent in advance. Contracts to use pipeline capacity or telecommunications bandwidth may require advance payments. Companies that use accrual accounting are able to postpone recognizing expenses.

Suppose, for example, that the company pays $120,000 rent up front for a year of access to a property. The cash in the company bank account is immediately lower, but the net worth of the company is not lower because the company has to access the facility. During the year, the company uses that access to the property to carry on business operations. At the end of the year, the company has no remaining right of future access, so that value is gone, and the company net worth is lower by $120,000 (all else being equal).

Under the cash basis of accounting, the company would post an expense of $120,000 when the payment is made:

RENT EXPENSE	$120,000	
CASH		$120,000

This method places a lump-sum expense at the beginning of the rental period and no expenses later. The balance sheet reflects no value for the prepaid use of the rental property.

In contrast, the accrual method recognizes that the cash payment represents an exchange of one asset (cash) for another (future use of the property). The transaction may be posted as:

PREPAID RENT	$120,000	
CASH		$120,000

The account PREPAID RENT is an asset that reflects the value of the future use of the rental property. Using the standard assumption of historical cost, the value of that access is equal to the price actually paid. The balance sheet will reflect this future value, and the income statement will not 'immediately show an expense for the rent. Accountants say that the expense has been deferred or capitalized. In everyday English we can say that the impact of the rental expense has been delayed.

Each month of the rental period, the company recognizes a portion of the $120,000 prepayment as a rental expense and reduces the value of the PREPAID RENT asset by an equal amount:

RENT EXPENSE $10,000
PREPAID RENT $10,000

Using the accrual method to spread the $120,000 payment out over the life of the lease, the income statement avoids the swings in profitability caused by the timing of this rental payment. For a going concern that can make good use of the property, the accrual of the rental expense makes the income statement more meaningful. The balance sheet includes a declining value of the future use of the property, which makes the balance sheet a better measure of the financial position of the company.

It is, admittedly, more typical for a landlord to charge monthly rent. As it turns out, the accrual accounting creates a pattern of expenses that match traditional monthly rent. It is, however, not important to match this more typical cash flow pattern. Rather, the account seeks to match the recognition of the expense to the benefits received.

A company may capitalize (that is, postpone recognizing expense and instead include on the balance sheet as an asset) a number of expenses. Following is a partial list of deferrable expenses:

Some Expenses that May Get Deferred

Prepaid rent

Prepaid insurance

Drilling/mineral rights

Access to pipeline

Professional retainers

Broadband capacity

The Downside to Deferring Expenses

In the preceding example, postponing the prepayment of rental expense probably makes both the income statement and balance sheet more useful to most readers of the financial statements. In this example, the accrual method better matches the expense to the production of revenue for the company. As a fringe benefit, the financial results of this company will be more comparable to the results of a company that has a lease with monthly payments.

Companies have improperly deferred expenses that should have been recognized as a way to overstate the net income of a company. If a company deferred or capitalized expenses in cases where there is no future service or other value to enjoy, then the company would understate current expenses and therefore overstate current income. The abuse of expense deferral would also overstate later expenses, which should have been recognized in a prior period.

Depreciation, Depletion, and Amortization: A Different Kind of Deferred Expense

Suppose XYZ Corporation bought an asset for $300,000. The asset should last 10 years. If the asset is a machine, XYZ will depreciate the machine. If the asset is a natural resource, XYZ will deplete the resource. If the asset is intangible, XYZ will amortize the value. These alternatives are described next.

The Asset Is a Machine   In Chapter 1, we saw that it is simple to account for the exchange of one asset for another (purchase with cash) or to acquire a new asset and assume a liability for future repayment.

Entries for the acquisition of the asset may look like the following:

A cash basis company might debit an expense account such as COST OF GOODS SOLD even though the machinery has an expected useful life of 10 years. They would recognize the entire purchase price as an expense:

COST OF GOODS SOLD	$10,000	
CASH		$10,000

Alternatively, an accrual-based customer may decide to treat the purchase of the machinery as an acquisition of an asset (machinery) in return for another asset (cash).

MACHINERY	$10,000	
CASH		$10,000

This method postpones recognizing income indefinitely. Perhaps when the equipment wears out, the accrual accountants might recognize an expense or loss on the equipment:

LOSS ON EQUIPMENT	$10,000	
MACHINERY		$10,000

If the equipment has some salvage value, the amounts to post may be a little more complicated but would follow the preceding patterns. Each of the methods postpones recognizing expenses for a time, then recognizes expenses on disposition of the equipment. None of the preceding methods meets the basic requirements of modern accounting because the timing of the revenues for the company is not matched to the expenses for the company.

Accountants use a method called depreciation to better match the revenues and expenses incurred to earn the revenue. Suppose the money spent to buy the equipment was spread out over the 10-year expected life of the equipment. The company needs to record the reduction in cash when the equipment is purchased. The company also creates an asset of equal value as presented in the entries above. In addition, the company recognizes $1,000 of expense in the form of wear and tear on the equipment each year. So, each year, the value of the equipment decreases and some of that value gets included in the income statement as an expense. After 10 years, the $10,000 has been included in the income statement, and the balance sheet reflects the decline in value of the machinery.

The actual entries to accomplish the preceding sequence do not follow the simplest and most intuitive pattern. Generally, the initial acquisition of the equipment looks logical enough:

1/2/20X1	MACHINERY	$10,000
1/2/20X1	CASH	$10,000

Then, at the end of one year, one tenth of the value is removed from the MACHINERY account and included as an expense. These entries do not follow the most obvious pattern:

12/31/20X1	DEPRECIATION EXPENSE	$1,000
12/31/20X1	ACCUMULATED DEPRECIATION	$1,000

The expense category DEPRECIATION EXPENSE is a place to hold the expenses that represent the loss in value over time and with use. As an expense, it represents a temporary account that will eventually reduce the net worth of the company. This expense reduces the income for each of the 10 years the company anticipates using the equipment.

The expense approximately matches the decline in value of the machinery. As seen earlier, however, the MACHINERY account is not altered. Instead, an "accumulation" account is created. Note that the $1,000 is a credit to this accumulation account instead of a credit to the MACHINERY account. At year-end, the MACHINERY account will still carry the machinery at cost ($10,000 as a debit) but will also contain a credit for $1,000. The ACCUMULATED DEPRECIATION account is a subtotal of the wear and tear on the machinery.

The ACCUMULATED DEPRECIATION account is an example of a "contra account." In this case, the account is an asset account, except that it acts as a way to reduce or cancel out other assets.

At the end of the year, the accounting records will still carry MACHINERY at $10,000 as a debit and also carry ACCUMULATED DEPRECIATION as a credit of $1,000. The balance sheet will probably net the two values and include the difference on the statement. Therefore, the balance sheet, which sums the value of assets and liabilities, will not be significantly impacted by the preceding accounting treatment. However, this method provides additional information that may be of use to some analysts.

Accountants use several methods to allocate the decline in value to different years. The simplest method is called the straight-line method, which allocates an equal amount of expense to each year.

To calculate the annual expense, the accountant needs to determine the useful life of the asset and the value at the end of that useful life. The value at the end of the useful life is called residual value or salvage value. The straight-line method allocates the decline from cost to the salvage value over the expected life.

Fractional periods are allocated in an intuitive manner. For example, if an asset is acquired halfway through the year, a fractional portion of a full year's expense is included in both the first and last years of the expected life.

If an asset is still productive after the passage of the original expected useful life, no additional expense is included for the bonus years. The value of the asset remains on the books, but the ACCUMULATED DEPRECIATION reduces the value to the assumed salvage value.

A second method that has historically been used by accountants is called the double-declining-balance method. The accountant again estimates the expected life of the asset. Then, a percentage decline is calculated solely from the expected life. For example, if the asset is expected to last 10 years, one tenth or 10 percent is the assumed decline in value in each year. For double-declining-balance, however, twice this amount is used. So, for an asset with an expected life of 10 years, depreciation equals 2 × 10 percent, or 20 percent of the depreciated value of the asset.

In using the double-declining-balance method, the salvage value of the asset is not used to determine the percentage. The depreciation is repeatedly applied to the shrinking asset value. At the point where the depreciated value of the asset would fall below the salvage value, depreciation is limited, so the value of the asset stops at the salvage value.

Double-declining-balance depreciation accelerates the recognition of DEPRECIATION EXPENSE. Recognizing expenses faster may provide tax benefits over lower deprecation methods. Although this accelerated method produces lower taxable income, at least in the earlier years, it does not necessarily produce lower financial profits on the company income statement. In fact, companies can use one method for financial reporting and another for tax reporting.

A third traditional way to account for the decline in value of a company asset is called sum of the years' digits. Suppose an asset is expected to last 5 years. Add up the numbers 1, 2, 3, 4, and 5. These numbers sum to 15. In the first year, 5/15 or 33 percent of the original asset value gets reported as depreciation. In the second year, 4/15 of the original cost gets reported as depreciation. And so forth. Accountants must be sure to avoid depreciating assets below their salvage value.

The most recently created commonly used accounting method is called the modified accelerated cost recovery system (MACRS). This accelerated path of depreciation is a series of depreciation schedules published by the Internal Revenue Service. Companies generally use MACRS depreciation for producing depreciation on their tax documents. Companies using MACRS for tax reporting often use straight-line depreciation for financial reporting.

The Asset Is a Natural Resource   Accountants follow the same philosophy when accounting for mineral rights or drilling rights, but the accounting entries are somewhat different than assets subject to depreciation.

In general, the depletion expense is calculated in the same way that depreciation is calculated. Companies frequently apply the straight-line method based on the total predicted amount of natural resources to be extracted.

Also, like depreciating assets, the value of the natural resource remains at the historical cost in the accounting records. Also like depreciating assets, an accumulation account is used to hold the decline in value that the accountants assume in preparing the income statement:

12/31/20X1	DEPLETION EXPENSE	$1,000	
12/31/20X1	ACCUMULATED DEPLETION		$1,000

The Asset Is an Intangible Asset Intangible assets may be subject to amortization rather than depreciation or depletion. Accountants handle intangible assets a bit differently. For example, as described in Chapter 3, goodwill is not amortized at all. Instead, the value of the goodwill remains unchanged unless the company determines that the value of the goodwill has declined, at which time the goodwill is revalued to the new amount.

Other intangible assets, such as patent and trademarks, are amortized over their useful life. Unlike depreciation expense and depletion expense, the amount of the amortization is not collected in an accumulation account. Instead, the expense reduces the value of the intangible asset:

12/31/20X1	AMORTIZATION EXPENSE	$1,000	
12/31/20X1	PATENT		$1,000

CONCLUSION

Accrual accounting permits accountants to determine the proper time to recognize revenues and expenses. The intention of accrual accounting is to make financial statements more meaningful. To be meaningful, accountants need to make reasonable assumptions that affect the timing of the revenues and expenses.

5.1. Revisit the June 22 transaction described in Question 4.3. Now, two additional provisions have been added—a commission and an allowance for nonpayment. You ship 3,500 NCDs on June 22 to OEM Communications for a gross price of $26 per unit to be paid within 30 days. A commission of 20 percent is payable to Lavalier Sales and Marketing (Channel Islands). Based on the prior experience of Lavalier Corporation, you predict that 3 percent of sales will be uncollectible.

5.2. Revisit the July 18 transaction described in Question 4.5. Now, the July 18 transaction must include the additional information provided in Question 5.1. You receive payment in full on July 18 for the June sales to OEM Communications. You pay the sales commission to Lavalier Sales and Marketing (Channel Islands) and keep the balance of the cash in your demand deposit account.

5.3. Recall in Question 1.6, you bought $45,000 of equipment on January 19. Your auditing firm advises you to use a four-year-life, zero residual value and suggests you use the straight-line method of depreciation. Your auditor believes it is acceptable to treat the current year as a full year for depreciation purposes. Enter the depreciation entries for 20X1 as a once-a-year entry on December 31.

5.4. On January 4, you hire four employees (including yourself) for salaries totaling $600,000 per year, payable monthly. However, 20 percent of the salaries are withheld for payroll taxes.

5.5. On each quarter-end (March 31, June 30, September 30, and December 31), the company files payroll tax forms and pays the withheld taxes to the federal government (for simplicity, assume there is no state tax or company portion of payroll taxes).

5.6. (*Note:* This question is presented out of sequence because the remaining questions are repetitious and hence presented in the section below.) You learn that Acme Electronics is in financial trouble. Acme owes you $288,750 for a sale on August 26. You agree to accept $242,000, which arrives on 10/15/X1. Currently, you carry $25,564 in the ALLOWANCE FOR UNCOLLECTIBLES account.

5.7. To complete the year, you calculate the amortization on the patents acquired on January 19 for $2 million. You decide that the patents had 10 years of useful life remaining when acquired.

5.8. Oops. It is early January 20X2. Although LCI received monthly statements from the bank, they haven't booked the interest income totaling $31,125.66 for 20X1. LCI accountants discuss the matter with LCI's auditor, who suggests they enter the total in one entry on 12/31/20X1 since LCI has not closed the books yet.

Note: The remaining questions and answers in this chapter reflect activities needed to describe sales that occur for the rest of the year. These questions and answers resemble transactions documented above.

5.9. You sell 9,500 NCDs on July 25 to Excellent Acoustics for $25.75 against a cash payment in full. Lavalier Sales and Marketing (Channel Islands) was not involved in the transaction, so no commission is payable. Despite the advance payment, you decide to expense for uncollectibles anyway.

5.10. You sell 11,000 NCDs on August 26 to Acme Electronics for $26.25 for payment in 30 days. Lavalier Sales and Marketing (Channel Islands) was not involved in the transaction, so no commission is payable. You maintain a 3 percent allowance for uncollectibles.

5.11. You ship 9,500 NCDs on September 22 to OEM Communications for a gross price of $27.50 per unit to be paid within 30 days. A commission of 20 percent is payable to Lavalier Sales and Marketing (Channel Islands). Based on the prior experience of Lavalier Corporation, you predict that 3 percent of the sale is uncollectible.

5.12. You sell 10,000 NCDs on October 25 to Excellent Acoustics for $26 against a cash payment in full. Lavalier Sales and Marketing (Channel Islands) was not involved in the transaction, so no commission is payable. Despite the advance payment, you decide to expense for uncollectibles anyway. You decide to reserve 4 percent of sales as uncollectible from now on.

5.13. You sell 10,000 NCDs on November 25 to Excellent Acoustics for $26 against a cash payment in full. Lavalier Sales and Marketing (Channel Islands) was not involved in the transaction, so no commission is payable. Despite the advance payment, you decide to expense for uncollectibles anyway. You reserve 4 percent of sales as uncollectible.

5.14. You sell 11,000 NCDs on December 28 to Zebutronics Communications for $26.50 with payment due in 30 days. No commission is payable.

5.15. On December 31, you receive the semiannual interest payment on the bond investment. You do not reinvest the interest from the December 31 payment in a new investment.

CHAPTER 6

The Statement of Cash Flows

All the journal entries are used to create either the balance sheet or the income statement. That is, every journal entry affects either the balance sheet or the income statement. The statement of cash flow (also called the statement of cash position) relies on the same financial accounting information to document changes in the cash position over the most recent accounting period. The statement of cash flows measures the sources and uses of cash.

IMPORTANCE OF CASH

Companies must manage cash to stay in business, to be able to pay bills on time, to satisfy present and future lenders, and to maximize the price of the common shares of the company.

Companies need cash to satisfy the short-term and longer-term needs of the business. Over the short term, companies must buy an array of goods and services to run their business properly. The company must buy materials, labor, and capital equipment. Companies can delay paying for these goods and services for a time but must pay in cash soon enough.

Young businesses may fail because they run out of cash. A company can experience a shortage of cash. Any business can experience financial challenges if it does not have the ability to generate sufficient cash to continue operating.

The securities markets and the banking industry can assist companies in managing their cash, including borrowing or investing cash to match the company's immediate needs. The financial markets can also assist the company to get through periods when a company's cash is inadequate. Both lenders and investors prefer a company that can generate cash needed for current operations and expansion.

AN INTUITIVE WAY TO TRACK CASH

Accountants could reanalyze journal entries to learn about what parts of the business are producing cash and what parts of the business are using cash. In a sense, such an analysis is not necessary. All the debits and credits already are included in the income statement and balance sheet, so the analysis of cash position is a supplemental report created to provide additional information.

Computers make it possible to review all the journal entries with an eye toward understanding the cash inflows and outflows. For example, it would be possible to identify all the sales entries (credit) for which the offsetting debit is an increase in cash. Likewise, the sales that are originally paired with accounts receivable require a different treatment. The computer would need to follow each sale to track how and when the customer ultimately paid the sales invoice.

Likewise, a cash management study could identify any purchase of raw materials, labor, or capital equipment paid immediately from cash. The total of all these transactions documents some of the ways a company spends cash. As with credit sales, the computer that reviewed the transactions would also need to track similar purchases of materials, labor, and capital offset by credits to a payable account, being aware of which transactions do and which do not affect cash.

The process could be described as follows: Identify and discard all pairs of debits and credits that do not affect cash at the time of the transaction or later. This leaves transactions that immediately involve cash flows and transactions involving receivables or payables where a future cash flow is anticipated.

We can see from Figure 6.1 that if we look at both the 2007 and 2008 balance sheets, accountants do not need to take a second pass through the data. All the data have been accumulated into either the income statement or the balance sheet. In fact, accountants use the income statement and the balance sheet to produce the statement of cash flows, rather than reanalyzing the data.

STANDARD ACCOUNTING CATEGORIES ON THE STATEMENT OF CASH FLOWS

The statement of cash flows includes three sections. The first section is generally described as results from operations in the current period. This section reflects changes in cash flow caused by the operation of the business. The second section reflects changes in the investments (including both

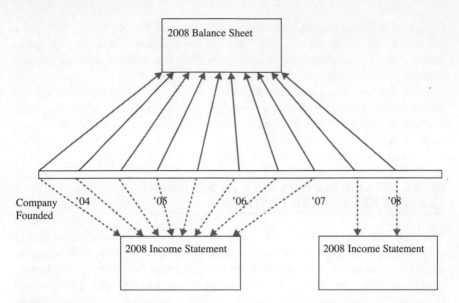

FIGURE 6.1 Time Line of Journaled Transactions Including Inputs to the Statement of Cash Flows

financial assets and firm production resources) the company makes. The final section reflects changes in the way the company finances the assets (through short-term and long-term debt and several kinds of equity).

The first section, the operations section, resembles the net income. It is tempting to believe that cash should rise by the profit the firm makes. Many factors complicate the relationship and those factors are the primary topic of this chapter. We have learned that companies have reasons to accelerate or slow down the recognition of revenues and expenses. The operating section of the statement of cash position essentially restates the income statement on a cash basis rather than an accrual basis adjusted for changes in a couple current assets on the balance sheet.

The second section, the investing section, documents the ways a company invests and divests. As a result, it accumulates the cash used to purchase new plant and equipment used in conducting business operations. This section also lists investments in longer term bonds and stock of other companies. Because the statement tracks sources and uses, this section also tracks sources of cash from sale of plant and equipment and cash invested in the securities of other companies, including bonds and stock.

The third section, the financing section, documents changes in ownership of the company, including both stock outstanding and bond borrowing. Sources include issuance of additional common stock, preferred stock, bonds, or warrants. Uses of cash include the repurchase of the company's stock, retiring preferred stock, or closing out warrants through expiration or exercise. The company also uses cash reported in the financing section when it pays dividends.

Companies may produce a statement of cash flows using either the indirect or direct method. Either method should result in identically the same sources and uses of cash within the operating, investing, and financing sections of the statement of cash flows.

USING THE INDIRECT METHOD TO DOCUMENT CHANGES IN THE CASH POSITION

The statement of cash flows contains three sections documenting how cash was generated or used in the operation of the company, how cash was generated or used in investments made by the company, and how cash was generated or used in financing the company. Both the indirect method (presented immediately below) and the direct method (presented later in this chapter) document the sources and uses of cash within these three areas.

Operating

The indirect method is commonly used by corporations. This method begins with net income from the income statement. This method takes net income as a starting estimate for changes in cash position and makes adjustment to incorporate reasons why net income does not correspond to cash flow.

The first adjustment adds back expenses that reduced net income but did not require cash. For most companies, the largest expense added back to income is depreciation. Depreciation is an expense created by accrual accounting that does not correspond to a draw on cash at the firm. As described in Chapter 5, depreciation approximates the erosion or wear and tear on manufacturing equipment, buildings, or other productive assets. Although the company often pays cash to acquire those assets, the assets may be acquired in a prior period and have no impact on cash flow in the current year. If the assets are acquired in the current period, the purchase of these assets is handled in the investing section described later in this chapter.

Depletion is similar to depreciation, except that it applies to mineral rights and similar land use contracts. Like depreciation, depletion is a noncash expense created by accountants to roughly match the erosion in value of the natural resources over the year. Although the company often pays cash to acquire those assets, the assets may be acquired in a prior period and have no impact on cash flow in the current year. If the assets are acquired in the current period, the purchase of these assets is handled in the investing section described later in this chapter.

Amortization is also similar to depreciation, except it applies to intangible assets. Like depreciation, amortization is a noncash expense created by accountants to roughly match the erosion in value of intangible assets over the year. Although the company often pays cash to acquire those assets, the assets may be acquired in a prior period and have no impact on cash flow in the current year. If the assets are acquired in the current period, the purchase of these assets is handled in the investing section described later in this chapter.

Companies may have additional noncash expenses that must be added back to net income in this section of the statement of cash flows. For example, when the company accrues bad debt expense or recognizes warranty expenses, accountants add back these expenses.

In addition, the indirect method accounts for changes on the balance sheet to document cash flows. For example, if our accounts receivables account increases from one year to the next, we are net lending more money to customers. The cash flow predicted from adjusted net income is further reduced by the increase in these trade credits.

Conversely, if a company owes additional money to suppliers from one year to the next, the company is, in effect, borrowing from suppliers. This trade credit is generally included in the operating section of the statement.

If the company increases (decreases) its investment in operating assets such as INVENTORY, the use (source) of cash is recorded in the operating section of the statement of cash flows.

Investing

The investing section includes transactions to buy assets such as equipment, land, and manufacturing facilities. Net new investment in INVENTORY or raw materials is included in the operating section.

The investing section also includes investments in longer-term fixed income and equity instruments of other companies. So, if a company invests in the bonds of another company, it is recorded as a use of cash in the investing section.

Likewise, a sale of plant and equipment shows up as a source of cash in the investing section. In addition, the sale of investments in the stock or bonds of other companies is a source of cash that is included in the investment section of the statement of cash flows.

Financing

In general, transactions involving the debt or equity of the company are included in the financing section of the statement of cash flows. If a company issues common stock, preferred stock, or bonds, the cash proceeds are recorded as a source of cash in the financing section.

Similarly, if the company buys back shares of stock, buys and retires bonds, or repays bonds at maturity, the cash outflow is recorded as a use of cash in the financing section of the statement of cash flows.

Dividends are cash payments made by companies to shareholders out of retained earnings. For this reason, dividend payments are recorded as a use of cash in the financing section of the statement of cash flows. Material non-cash transactions should be disclosed in footnotes to the statement of cash flows.

Noncash Transactions

Some transactions do not involve cash. For example, if a company exchanges common stock to acquire land, neither the debit to land nor the credit to common equity affect cash. These types of transactions are not common for a modern cash-based business. Still, when these transactions occur, they are generally omitted from the statement of cash flows. Material non-cash transactions should be disclosed in footnotes to the statement of cash flows.

USING THE DIRECT METHOD TO DOCUMENT CHANGES IN THE CASH POSITION

The direct method is often considered more descriptive and potentially a more useful source of information about the cash flow of a company than the indirect method. Only the operating section of the statement of cash flows differs between the direct method and the indirect method.

Operating

The two major sections of the operating section of the statement of cash flow are CASH RECEIPTS and CASH PAYMENTS. As with the indirect method described above, the direct method measures the cash flow from the business.

The major receipts are payments received from customers. The starting amount for the cash received is generally SALES (revenues). In fact, revenues must be reduced by the increase in accounts receivables, bad debt expense, and the increase in bad debit, allowance.

Of course, customers may immediately pay cash, but many companies record a sale before the cash is received. Most of the accounts receivable is paid during the year, so it is necessary to add (subtract) only a small adjustment to account for the increase (decrease) in accounts receivable. The increase or decrease in the ACCOUNTS RECEIVABLE account equals the change in the amount carried on the balance sheet from one year to the next.

The company must also reduce the sales receipts for write-offs of uncollectable accounts receivable. Companies estimate and accrue bad debt expense. The income statement reports the accrued expenses during the period, but the cash receipts are overstated by the actual write-offs. The actual loss on the accounts receivable equals accrued expense less (plus) the increase (decrease) in the allowance for uncollectable. The increase or decrease in the ALLOWANCE FOR UNCOLLECTIBLE account equals the change in the amount carried on the balance sheet from one year to the next.

A second cash receipt includes interest and dividends received. Because most companies accrue income, it may be necessary to adjust the INTEREST INCOME account on the income statement downward (upward) by the increase (decrease) in ACCRUED INTEREST appearing on the balance sheet at the end of the year compared to the beginning of the year.

Dividends do not accrue over time, but it is possible that the company recognized dividends declared but not yet paid. In practice, companies do not tend to pay dividends near the end of the year, so dividends probably require no adjustment for companies with fiscal years that end on December 31.

Cash receipts are summarized in Equation 6.1:

$$
\begin{aligned}
\text{CASH RECEIPTS} = \ &\text{REVENUES} \\
&+ \text{ACCOUNTS RECEIVABLE} \\
&- \text{UNCOLLECTIBLE EXPENSE} \\
&+ \text{ALLOWANCE FOR UNCOLLECTIBLES} \\
&+ \text{INTEREST and DIVIDENDS received}
\end{aligned}
\tag{6.1}
$$

In addition to receipts, the operating section of the statement of cash flows calculated using the direct method must account for payments. For most businesses, the major payments are made to supplies. The statement of cash flows for companies using the direct method lists these just after receipts.

The direct method begins with COST OF GOODS SOLD expense from the income statement. Most of the cash actually paid to suppliers is first recorded as INVENTORY (including raw materials and finished goods), so the actual amount is not recognized on the income statement directly. During the year, the company sells and replenishes the INVENTORY, so the statement of cash flows adds (subtracts) the increase (decrease) in INVENTORY. This net change in INVENTORY requires cash payments not included in the COST OF GOODS SOLD.

The direct method must also adjust the payments for ACCOUNTS PAYABLE. The company may pay cash immediately to some of its suppliers. Other purchases are matched to credits to ACCOUNTS PAYABLE instead of CASH. The company pays many of those bills over the year, so the impact on cash is the change in ACCOUNTS PAYABLE. The direct method subtracts (adds) the increase (decrease) in ACCOUNTS PAYABLE.

The direct method includes several adjustments for payments to general and administrative employees and the payment of income tax. Obviously, labor costs included in the COST OF GOODS SOLD are not included again here. Also, the income statement reports the accrued payments for administrative employees and accrued income taxes, not the actual cash amounts paid.

The direct method also accounts for interest paid (but not dividends paid). The INTEREST EXPENSE on the income statement is adjusted downward (upward) for changes in ACCRUED INTEREST PAYABLE.

Cash payments are summarized in Equations 6.2 through 6.4:

$$\text{Cash Payments to Suppliers} = \text{COST OF GOODS SOLD} \\ + \text{INVENTORY} \qquad (6.2) \\ - \text{ACCOUNTS PAYABLE}$$

$$\text{Cash Payments for Operating Expenses} = \text{OPERATING EXPENSES} \\ + \text{PREPAID EXPENSES} \\ - \text{ACCRUED EXPENSES} \\ \text{PAYABLE} \\ (6.3)$$

$$\text{Cash Payments for Income Taxes} = \\ + \text{INCOME TAX EXPENSE} \quad (6.4) \\ - \text{INCOME TAX PAYABLE}$$

where Δ {account} represents the change in a balance sheet account during the year.

Investing

The transactions described in the indirect method involving the investing section of the statement of cash flows are handled the same way under the direct method.

Financing

The transactions described in the indirect method involving the financing section of the statement of cash flows are handled the same way under the direct method.

Table 6.1 reprints the balance sheet introduced in Chapter 3 as Table 3.1 and Table 6.2 reprints the income statement introduced in Chapter 4 as Table 4.1 for Lavaliere Industries. The balance sheet amounts, changes in the balance sheet amounts, and values off the income statement

TABLE 6.1 Balance Sheet: Lavaliere Industries, December 31, 20X2 ($000)

ASSETS	20X1	20X2	Difference
	20X1	20X2	Difference
CASH	$133,000	$ 66,000	$67,000
ACCOUNTS RECEIVABLE	70,000	60,000	10,000
MERCHANDISE INVENTORY	30,000	20,000	10,000
PREPAID EXPENSES	5,000	2,000	3,000
LAND	200,000	100,000	100,000
BUILDINGS	320,000	130,000	190,000
ACCUMULATED DEPRECIATION— BLDG	(22,000)	(10,000)	(12,000)
EQUIPMENT	54,000	20,000	34,000
ACCUMULATED DEPRECIATION— EQUIPMENT	(6,000)	(2,000)	(4,000)
TOTAL ASSETS	$784,000	$386,000	
LIABILITIES AND SHAREHOLDERS' EQUITY			
ACCOUNTS PAYABLE	56,000	24,000	32,000
INCOME TAX PAYABLE	12,000	16,000	(4,000)
BONDS PAYABLE	160,000	125,000	35,000
COMMON STOCK	180,000	125,000	55,000
RETAINED EARNINGS	376,000	96,000	280,000
TOTAL LIABILITIES AND SHAREHOLDERS' EQUITY			
	$784,000	$386,000	

TABLE 6.2 Income Statement: Lavaliere Industries for the Year Ending 20X2 ($000)

REVENUES		$1,014,000
INTEREST INCOME		24,000
COST OF GOODS SOLD	300,000	
OPERATING EXPENSES (includes $18,000 DEPRECIATION)	240,000	
INTEREST EXPENSE	84,000	
LOSS ON SALE OF EQUIPMENT	6,000	630,000
INCOME BEFORE INCOME TAXES		408,000
INCOME TAX EXPENSE		94,000
NET INCOME		$ 314,000

will be used to generate a statement of cash flows using both the indirect method and the direct method.

PRODUCING A STATEMENT OF CASH FLOWS USING THE INDIRECT METHOD

The indirect method begins with NET INCOME and makes adjustments for noncash items on the income statement. Then, changes in balance sheet accounts will explain other changes in the operating section. Changes in balance sheet accounts will be used to measure cash in the investing and financing sections. A line-by-line explanation of the calculations follows Table 6.3.

The indirect method begins with NET INCOME of $314,000. This value comes directly off the bottom line of the Lavaliere income statement. Next, noncash expenses are added back. Depreciation of $18 million is identified on the Lavaliere income statement. Other noncash accrued expenses, such as accrued write-offs held in ALLOWANCE FOR UNCOLLECTIBLES (not indicated on these statements) would also be added back.

The statement next adds back losses that were recognized on the income statement because they reduce reported income but not cash. The company reported a loss of $6 million on the sale of equipment. Similarly, gains that might appear on the income statement would be subtracted because they do increase reported income but produce no cash.

Next, a series of changes in operating assets and liabilities are included. Lavaliere reduced the amount it owed suppliers by $10 million (comparing ACCOUNTS PAYABLES in 20X2 versus 20X1), which required $10 million in cash not included in the income statement. According to its balance sheet, Lavaliere also increased MERCHANDISE INVENTORY. The

TABLE 6.3 Statement of Cash Flows (Indirect Method): Lavaliere Industries for the Year Ending 20X1 ($000)

Cash Flow from Operating Activities		
NET INCOME		$314,000
Adjustments:		
DEPRECIATION EXPENSES	18,000	
Loss on Sale of Equipment	6,000	
Decrease in ACCOUNTS RECEIVABLES	(10,000)	
Increase in MERCHANDISE INVENTORY	(10,000)	
Increase in PREPAID EXPENSES	(3,000)	
Increase in ACCOUNTS PAYABLE	32,000	
Decrease in INCOME TAX PAYABLE	(4,000)	29,000
Net Cash Provided by Operating Activities		$343,000
Cash Flows from Investing Activities		
Purchase of Building	(190,000)	
Purchase of Equipment	(50,000)	
Sale of Equipment	8,000	
Purchase of Land	(100,000)	
Net Cash Used by Investing Activities	(332,000)	
Cash Flows from Financing Activities		
Issuance of Common Stock	$ 55,000	
Issuance of Debt	35,000	
Payment of Cash Dividends	(34,000)	
Net Cash Used by Financing Activities	56,000	
Net Increase in Cash	67,000	
Cash at the Beginning of the Period	66,000	
`Cash at the End of the Period	$133,000	

statement subtracts the $10 million paid to purchase additional inventory. For example, PREPAID EXPENSES on the balance sheet rose by $3 million, from $2 million to $5 million. The increase required $3 million in cash and is subtracted from the adjusted cash balance. Lavaliere increased the amount of money owed to suppliers (ACCOUNTS PAYABLE) by $32 million, from $24 million to $56 million as reported on the Lavaliere balance sheet. Finally, the company reduced the stated liability for taxes on its balance sheet by $4 million (from $16 million to $12 million) presumably by paying $4 million more in cash than income tax expenses reported on the income statement.

The impact of operating activities on cash equals NET INCOME of $314 million plus $18 million noncash DEPRECIATION EXPENSE plus an additional $29 million in CASH generated by changes in operating assets and liabilities, for a net contribution of $343 million CASH.

The second section of the indirect statement of cash flows lists investing activity for Lavaliere Industries. The company used $190 million to purchase a new building or buildings. The balance sheet shows the investment because the amount in the BUILDINGS account rose from $130 million to $320 million. The company also spent $50 million on EQUIPMENT, although the value of EQUIPMENT on the balance sheet rose by only $34 million from $20 million to $54 million because of other EQUIPMENT sold and retired. Likewise, we rely on other information to know that the sale of other equipment generated $8 million. Finally, the balance sheet documents the purchase of LAND costing $100 million because the company carried $100 million in land in 20X1 and $200 million in land in 20X2.

The financing section documents that Lavaliere issued $55 million in common stock, as the balance sheet amount of paid-in common rose from $125 million to $180 million. The cash produced is included as a source of cash. The company also issued debt for proceeds of $35 million ($125 million in debt on the balance sheet for 20X1 rose to $160 million for 20X2). The company must have paid $34 million in dividends because the RETAINED EARNINGS rose from $96 million to $376 million, $34 million less than the NET INCOME of $314 million.

The balance sheet CASH balance increased by $67 million, from $66 million at year-end 20X1 to $133 million at year-end 20X2. The net CASH provided by operations ($343 million) plus the net cash used by investing activities ($332 million) plus net cash flow from investing also totaled $67 million.

PRODUCING A STATEMENT OF CASH FLOWS USING THE DIRECT METHOD

The direct statement of cash flows begins with REVENUES and subtracts off COST OF GOODS SOLD. Although this sounds similar to the indirect method, the direct method combines information from individual income and balance sheet items to construct sources and uses of cash. A line-by-line explanation of the calculations follows Table 6.4.

The largest source of cash for most companies is SALES or SERVICE REVENUE. Lavaliere produces $1.004 billion receipts from customers. The company recognized $1.014 billion of revenue on the income statement. However, the company's ACCOUNTS RECEIVABLE rose by $10 million, indicating that the company actually collected $1,004 billion.

Lavaliere also received INTEREST INCOME of $24 million. Perhaps the company earned ACCRUED INCOME that differed slightly from actual interest paid. However, the company shows no interest accruals, so the accrued interest is apparently not material.

TABLE 6.4 Statement of Cash Flows (Direct Method): Lavaliere Industries for the Year Ending 20X1 ($000)

Cash Flow from Operating Activities		
Sources of Cash:		
Cash Receipts from Customers	$1,004,000	
Interest Received	24,000	1,028,000
Uses of Cash:		
To Suppliers	278,000	
For Operating Expenses	225,000	
For Interest	84,000	
For Income Taxes	98,000	685,000
Net Cash Provided by Operating Activities	343,000	
Cash Flows from Investing Activities		
Purchase of Building	(190,000)	
Purchase of Equipment	(50,000)	
Sale of Equipment	8,000	
Purchase of Land	(100,000)	
Net Cash Used by Investing Activities	(332,000)	
Cash Flows from Financing Activities		
Issuance of Common Stock	$ 55,000	
Issuance of Debt	35,000	
Payment of Cash Dividends	(34,000)	
Net Cash Used by Financing Activities	56,000	
Net Increase in Cash	67,000	
Cash at the Beginning of the Period	66,000	
Cash at the End of the Period	$ 133,000	

Lavaliere paid suppliers $278 million. The direct method begins with the COST OF GOODS SOLD of $300 million from the income statement and subtracts the $32 million increase in ACCOUNTS PAYABLE shown on the balance sheet and adds the additional $10 million in MERCHANDISE INVENTORY also documented on the balance sheet.

A second use of cash on the direct statement is a category that begins with operating expenses of $240 million, as reported on the Lavaliere income statement. Those operating expenses include $18 million of depreciation expense. The noncash depreciation expense is subtracted from the $240 million reported number. Lavaliere also prepaid $3 million in expenses as the balance in prepaid expenses rose from $2 million in 20X1 to $5 million in 20X2. The direct statement of cash flows includes this use of cash in this section of payments for operating expenses.

The next use of cash on the operating section of the direct statement of cash flows is interest expense. The income statement reports $84 million of interest expense. No information is available about interest accrued but not paid. If the company accrued a material amount of interest expense, the cash payment would be reduced by the change in the accrual carried on the balance sheet.

The final use of cash in the operating section of the direct statement of cash flows is income tax expense. The income statement reported income tax expense of $94 million. However, the balance sheet reveals that income tax payable declined by $4 million from $16 million in 20X1 to $12 million in 20X2. Therefore, the company used $98 million for income taxes in the year 20X2.

The cash flow from operations equals $343 million. Table 6.4 shows that the company received $1.028 billion in cash payments from customers and made $685 million payments. The cash flow from operations section using the indirect method in Table 6.3 and the direct method in Table 6.4 document the same $343 million cash supplied by operations.

The section documenting cash flows from investing activities and the section documenting cash flows from financing activities are identical to the investing and financing sections using the indirect method. Those sections are printed in Table 6.3 and repeated in Table 6.4. The calculations are described for Table 6.3.

Likewise, the reconciliation of beginning cash to ending cash and the cash reported on the balance sheet is identical on both the direct method in Table 6.4 and the indirect method in Table 6.3 because the cash documented in each of the three sections is equal.

CONCLUSION

All of the accounting entries made by a company enter either the income statement or the balance sheet. Because these two financial statements already tally up all the transactions that affect cash, accountants rely on values published in these two financial statements to document cash flows in the statement of cash flows. The statement of cash flows documents how cash is generated and how it is used for current operations, because of investments made or redeemed or because of financing activities.

6.1. Produce a statement of cash flows for Lavalier Communications, Inc. using the indirect method and the account totals from the trial balance below.

6.2. Produce a statement of cash flows for Lavalier Communications, Inc. using the direct method and the account totals from the trial balance below.

General Journal

Note: The account totals below were separately provided in Question 3.1 in Chapter 3 and Question 4.7 in Chapter 4.

Account	Debits	Credits
CASH	$6,490,001	$5,433,450
SECURITY DEPOSITS	4,000	0
ADVANCES TO SUPPLIERS	250,000	250,000
ACCOUNTS RECEIVABLE	932,500	641,000
ALLOWANCE FOR UNCOLLECTIBLES	25,564	59,029
FINISHED GOODS INVENTORY	650,000	645,000
PREPAID RENT	4,000	4,000
INVESTMENT IN BONDS	2,000,000	0
EQUIPMENT	45,000	0
ACCUMULATED DEPRECIATION	0	11,250
PATENTS	2,000,000	200,000
ACCOUNTS PAYABLE	215,450	315,450
PAYROLL TAXES PAYABLE	120,000	120,000
COMMON STOCK	0	1,000,000
PAID-IN CAPITAL IN EXCESS OF PAR	0	4,000,000
SALES REVENUE	0	1,697,125
INTEREST REVENUE	$ 0	$ 131,126

(*Continued*)

Account	Debits	Credits
COST OF GOODS SOLD	645,000	0
SALARY EXPENSE	480,000	0
COMMISSION EXPENSE	70,450	0
PAYROLL TAX EXPENSE	120,000	0
RENT EXPENSE	44,000	0
UNCOLLECTIBLE ACCOUNT EXPENSE	80,215	0
DEPRECIATION EXPENSE—EQUIPMENT	11,250	0
AMORTIZATION EXPENSE—PATENTS	200,000	0
PATENT LICENSE EXPENSE	$ 120,000	$ 0

CHAPTER 7

Ensuring Integrity

Companies go through many steps to ensure that financial statements are accurate, complete, and fair. Users of financial statements should also take steps to have a basis for relying on financial statements.

INTERNAL CONTROLS AND PROCEDURES

Companies take steps internally to ensure the integrity of their accounting records. Most companies are committed to growing their business honestly. Dishonest or incompetent employees pose a threat to the success of the company.

Articles in the financial press make clear that some companies would manipulate financial statements. In the absence of pressure from independent auditors, readers of financial statements, or regulatory organizations, some companies might be tempted to publish inaccurate or misleading financial statements. If a company failed to create a legitimate internal audit, they would find it difficult to produce audited financial statements.

Most of the recent disputes about the accuracy of financial records involve the way that business transactions are recorded. Bernard Madoff pleaded guilty to charges of fraud for creating false accounting records. Satyam Computer Systems announced that its founder, Ramalinga Raju, had also created fraudulent accounting records.

However, internal controls can usually make it difficult to create fraudulent entries. More commonly, accounting numbers are challenged by investors or regulators that argue that actual business transactions were included in the accounting records in an unfair or misleading manner.

Removing Opportunities for Fraud

As companies grow, managers should divide responsibilities to remove improper incentives. For example, people with the authority to withdraw cash should not be in charge of accounting for those withdrawals.

Companies also seek to automate record keeping. By automating the process of accounting for activity in the business, businesses can create more accurate inputs at lower cost that are less vulnerable to manipulation.

Create an Audit Trail

One of the most important things that internal control can do is to make sure there is documentation for the entries in the accounting records. A trail that independent auditors can follow to verify the accounting entries greatly improves the chances that improper accounting can be detected. By improving the chance of detection, internal procedures should also discourage attempts to create fraudulent entries.

INDEPENDENT AUDITING

Independent auditors can reduce the chance that a company's financial records are unfair or misleading. Audits look for evidence that the company has entered all relevant financial transactions into accounting records, that the entries represent real business transactions, and that the financial records comply with generally accepted accounting principles (GAAP).

Verifying Entries

Auditors use a number of techniques to verify that the company has created a complete and accurate set of journal entries. Auditors can check for completeness and accuracy by comparing accounting records to physical documents such as invoices and shipping records. Auditors can also spot check reported transactions by confirming a sampling of transactions with customers and suppliers.

Verifying Accounting Procedures

Independent auditors review the procedures and assumptions used by the company to complete financial reports. The auditors are responsible for confirming that the company has complied with GAAP.

Independent auditors should also detect situations where accounting procedures were not followed consistently. The auditors will determine that changes in accounting procedures do not create financial statements that are misleading.

THE ROLE OF THE USER OF FINANCIAL STATEMENTS

Users of financial statements have some responsibility to review the statements carefully. Users should actually read the statements, footnotes, comments from management, and additional supplemental disclosures if that information is important to them. In other words, users should not assume that the contents of financial statements are benign just because they are audited.

Users of financial statements should be mindful of who prepared the financial statements and who audited them. There are a number of firms that are qualified to audit financial statements. The largest accounting firms instill confidence. Medium-sized firms may be especially skilled at accounting for particular industries. Smaller firms may also have special skills that argue for relying on them. However, the smaller firms have fewer financial resources if they are found negligent in conducting their audit. If a small, unknown firm acts as auditor, users of financial statements should determine if the auditor was chosen because of special skills or because they were willing to accept a company's questionable accounting procedures.

Following is a list of things a user of financial statements should consider. In each case, the user is encouraged to consider how accounting assumptions may have affected the financial results.

Accrual Assumptions

A company can comply with GAAP and still have some opportunity to manipulate financial results. The company will disclose many facts about how they compiled their financial results. If the financial statements are audited, it is reasonable to assume that the published statements comply with GAAP rules and that an audit did not reveal any material errors.

Nevertheless, the company can make many decisions that can affect the timing of revenues and expenses. These choices create the opportunity to manipulate financial results.

Accelerating Revenues

Changes in accounting methods to recognize revenues sooner will lead to higher reported earnings over the near term followed by lower earnings later. Companies adopt new accounting methods to hide deteriorating results. Companies have some flexibility to pick accounting methods that show the company in a favorable light. But if the change reflects an effort to cover up unfavorable results, then readers of financial statements should be cautious.

Accelerating Expenses

Changing accounting methods to recognize expenses sooner will lead to lower reported earnings over the near term and higher earnings later. Companies may adopt new accounting methods in good times to build a cushion for later periods. Companies already showing poor results may also want to make things look as bad as possible so they can report positive results later.

Deferring Revenues

Much like accelerating expenses, changing accounting methods to defer revenues will lead to lower reported earnings over the near term and higher earnings later. Companies may adopt new accounting methods in good times to build a cushion for later periods. Companies already showing poor results may also want to make things look as bad as possible so they can report positive results later.

Deferring Expenses

Changes in accounting methods to defer expenses will lead to higher reported earnings over the near term followed by lower earnings later.

Companies adopt new accounting methods to hide deteriorating results. Companies have some flexibility to pick accounting methods that show the company in a favorable light. But if the change reflects an effort to cover up unfavorable results, then readers of financial statements should be cautious.

CONCLUSION

From time to time, newspapers report examples of companies that have defrauded investors or lenders by producing fraudulent or misleading financial statements. Of course, the newspapers do not report the countless instances where companies report fair and accurate financial results. When internal procedures are properly designed, when financial statements are thoroughly audited by independent auditors, and when readers of the financial statements review the published results critically, the chance to succeed is greatly reduced.

7.1. Suppose LCI accountants have made several mistakes in entering some accounting transactions. The company determines that they entered a particular debit twice in January, entered a debit as a credit in March, and failed to enter anything for a business transaction in May. Should the company edit and correct the entries in the database?

7.2. The financial statements of two companies reveal that one company has made many accounting assumptions that have the effect of raising profitability. In contrast, the second company does not seem to have adopted accounting conventions that lead to higher profitability. How can you compare the financial statements of the two companies?

7.3. How can a company ensure the integrity of their records if automated data entry has removed the "paper trail"?

CHAPTER 8

Financial Statement Analysis

This overview of financial analysis demonstrates how financial information is used and why it is valuable. This introduction will seek to motivate the reader to study financial statements more carefully and to begin to focus on information that may be drawn from the statements that go beyond the mechanical production of accounting results.

RESTATING ACCOUNTING RESULTS

Companies can make many choices when creating these financial records that may materially affect the balance sheet, income statement, and financial ratios. In addition, companies will have nonrecurring items that also affect one company's results in a particular year. To make comparisons between companies meaningful, financial statement analysis may begin by restating the results of all the companies to be consistent. To make the comparisons over time, financial analysts need to remove nonrecurring items from the adjusted financial results.

The footnotes provide a considerable amount of detail that can be used to restate financial results. Additional material may be found in other filings, news releases, or by asking the company for additional details.

Many of these adjustments require a detailed review of the accounting methods used by the individual companies. The adjustments may involve aspects of accounting not covered in this text, such as accounting for leases, pensions, minority interests, consolidated operations, and currency and other international issues.

RATIO ANALYSIS

One of the techniques used by analysts to study financial statements begins by constructing a number of ratios. Analysts combine numbers from income statements, balance sheets, and other disclosures to create measures of performance. An organized collection of ratios with formulas and a short description of each ratio follow.

Liquidity Ratios

The current ratio divides the current assets (assets that are likely to be consumed or converted to cash within a year) by the current liabilities (debt that is likely to be repaid or refinanced within a year). Both the current assets and current liabilities appear on the balance sheet.

The current ratio:

$$\text{Current Ratio} = \frac{\text{Current Assets}}{\text{Current Liabilities}} \qquad (8.1)$$

If current assets equal current liabilities, then the current ratio equals 1. The timing of the cash requirements of the current liabilities may not exactly match the timing of the assets available. Nevertheless, a current ratio of 1 has been viewed as typical and prudent.

The amount of liquidity necessary differs from company to company. Companies with seasonal or unpredictable cash flow may want to carry more current assets than a company that consistently generates positive cash flows.

Companies faced unanticipated demands for liquidity in 2008 and 2009 when many companies experienced sharply deteriorating cash flows and challenges in rolling over existing debt.

The quick ratio or acid test ratio:

$$\text{Quick Ratio} = \frac{\text{Cash} + \text{Short-Term Investments} + \text{Accounts Receivables}}{\text{Current Liabilities}}$$

$$(8.2)$$

The quick ratio excludes inventories and prepaid expenses from the numerator. For this reason, the quick ratio will generally be lower than 1. In most market conditions, accounts receivable can be sold or financed readily. The quick ratio is a more conservative measure of short-term liquidity than the current ratio.

In 2008–2009, the asset-backed market was disrupted by turmoil in the mortgage market and by losses in the banking and broker-dealer community. At times, companies may have had little ability to generate cash from accounts receivable. In addition, some short-term assets became illiquid. Some short-term investments declined significantly in value. In these market conditions, the quick ratio may not represent an acid test.

The accounts receivable turnover ratio:

$$\text{Accounts Receivable Turnover} = \frac{\text{Net Credit Sales}}{\text{Average Net Accounts Receivable}} \quad (8.3)$$

The accounts receivable turnover ratio measures how effectively a company generates sales relative to the credit extended to customers. The net credit sales in the numerator excludes cash sales and may be adjusted for returns and discounts. The accounts receivable in the denominator may be reduced by accrued losses due to collection problems. The accounts receivable is often an average of the beginning and ending accounts receivable balance. Where companies have large seasonal patterns in their accounts receivable, another way to average the accounts receivable may be desirable if the data needed to calculate the average is available.

A higher ratio is desirable because the accounts receivable generally doesn't earn interest, so there is a cost to carrying receivables. However, credit sales may be profitable sales even if the customers are slow to pay, so accepting a lower accounts receivable turnover ratio may be necessary to make profitable sales.

A low ratio may also indicate that the company has not been successful in getting paid by customers. A declining ratio may indicate general weakness in the economy or poor management of collection.

Days' sales in receivables:

$$\text{Days' Sales in Receivables} = \frac{\text{Average Net Accounts Receivable}}{\text{One Day's Sales}} \quad (8.4)$$

The days' sales in receivables ratio is similar to the accounts receivable turnover ratio. The accounts receivable turnover ratio puts SALES in the numerator and ACCOUNTS RECEIVABLE in the denominator. The days' sales in receivables puts ACCOUNTS RECEIVABLE in the numerator and SALES in the denominator. Annual sales are divided by 365, so the ratio roughly measures the average time to collect after a sale.

A low number of days is desirable. A high number may indicate that the company is not being effective in collecting from customers. However, profitable sales may require a company to accept delayed payment, so a higher ratio may not be a sign of poor collection efforts.

The inventory turnover ratio:

$$\text{Inventory Turnover} = \frac{\text{Cost of Goods Sold}}{\text{Average Inventory}} \quad (8.5)$$

The inventory turnover ratio divides cost of goods sold by inventory. The inventory used in the denominator is often the average of beginning and ending inventory. If the company is growing rapidly, using average inventory in the denominator may provide more meaningful results. Where companies have large seasonal patterns in their inventory, another way to average the inventory may be desirable if the data needed to calculate the average is available.

When a company makes a sale, it debits COST OF GOODS SOLD and credits INVENTORY. The company replaces the inventory and (hopefully) sells the inventory again and again. A higher ratio indicates that the company has been successful in selling inventory quickly.

Profitability Ratios

The return-on-assets ratio measures the profitability of the assets deployed by the firm. The total assets in the denominator are frequently the average of the beginning total assets and the ending total assets. Because the total assets are financed with either debt or equity, the denominator can be viewed as the investment base. The numerator includes net income, which is the profit available to the equity owners after expenses, including interest expense, have been paid. The sum of net income and interest expense is the combined return that the debt and equity holders earned.

The return-on-assets ratio:

$$\text{Return on Assets} = \frac{\text{Net Income} + \text{Interest Expense}}{\text{Average Total Assets}} \qquad (8.6)$$

The return on assets measures the profitability of the assets before the impact of leverage (borrowing). A higher return on assets is always desirable, but some businesses are in industries with higher return on assets and other businesses are in industries with lower return on assets.

The return-on-equity ratio:

$$\text{Return on Equity} = \frac{\text{Net Income} - \text{Preferred Dividends}}{\text{Average Equity}} \qquad (8.7)$$

The return-on-equity ratio divides the net income available to common shareholders by the average equity. If a company has preferred stock, the dividend must be paid on the preferred shares before the company can pay a dividend to common shareholders. The denominator may average the beginning equity and the ending equity. Generally, the equity is the book value of equity on the financial statements, not the market value of the shares.

A higher return on equity is always desirable. Investors look for consistency in the return as well. Companies with more volatile earnings may have a higher return-on-equity ratio over time, so investors may have to trade off the more desirable high return against the higher risk.

The gross profit ratio or gross profit percentage:

$$\text{Gross Profit Percentage} = \frac{\text{Gross Profit}}{\text{Net Sales Revenue}} \qquad (8.8)$$

The gross profit percentage divides the gross profit by net sales revenue. Sales revenue may be reduced by returns and allowances in industries that experience significant returns.

The gross profit percentage measures the percent of net sales that is available to cover administrative costs and overhead. A high gross profit percentage means that, as volume increases to more than cover these fixed costs, net income should rise rapidly as volume advances.

Companies with high gross profit may have patent protection, a technological advantage over competitors, or be operating in a sector experiencing rapid growth. Often, companies that earn a high gross profit percentage have a short product life cycle, so they must make a return on product design costs rapidly.

The profit margin or return-on-sales ratio:

$$\text{Profit Margin} = \text{Return on Sales} = \frac{\text{Net Income}}{\text{Net Sales}} \qquad (8.9)$$

The profit margin resembles the gross profit percentage except that net income is substituted in the numerator for gross profit. Net income subtracts operating expenses, interest, and income taxes from gross profit. Net income will be sensitive to volume compared to gross profit percentage.

The asset turnover ratio:

$$\text{Asset Turnover} = \frac{\text{Net Sales}}{\text{Average Total Assets}} \qquad (8.10)$$

Asset turnover divides net sales by average total assets. As above, sales may be reduced by returns and allowances if that adjustment is material. The total assets in the denominator average the total assets at the beginning of the period with total assets at the end.

The asset turnover ratio in combination with the gross profit percentage for profit margin can provide an indication of the profitability of the business. The asset turnover ratio measures the extent the company is deploying its assets effectively to produce sales while the gross profit percentage and the profit margin measure how profitable those sales are to the company.

Earnings per share (EPS):

$$\text{EPS} = \frac{\text{Net Income} - \text{Preferred Dividends}}{\text{Weighted Average Shares Outstanding}} \qquad (8.11)$$

Earnings per share equals the net income available for distribution to common shareholders divided by the number of shares outstanding. The net income available to common shareholders begins with net income and subtracts the dividends due to preferred stock shareholders. The weighted average number of shares outstanding takes into account changes in the number of shares outstanding during the year.

Fully diluted earnings per share:

$$\text{Fully Diluted EPS} = \frac{\text{Net Income} - \text{Preferred Dividends}}{\text{Total Shares Potentially Outstanding}} \qquad (8.12)$$

The fully diluted earnings per share is similar to the earnings-per-share calculation listed in Equation 8.11. Fully diluted earnings per share divides the net income in excess of preferred dividends by the number of shares that would be outstanding if all stock options and warrants outstanding were exercised and converted into common stock.

Solvency Ratios

The debt ratio, also called the debt-to-total-assets ratio, divides the debt by total assets. Since total assets also equals debt plus equity, it is convenient to think of the debt ratio as the percentage of the company financed by debt.

The debt ratio:

$$\text{Debt Ratio} = \text{Debt to Total Assets} = \frac{\text{Total Liabilities}}{\text{Total Assets}} \qquad (8.13)$$

Companies with a high debt ratio effectively leverage the equity holders' interest in the assets of the firm. Having a large amount of debt increases the risk that the net income will not be adequate to pay the interest expense on the debt. However, if the company earns enough to pay the interest, the equity holders benefit rapidly from additional increases in profit, as shareholders keep a higher percentage of the increase in profit.

The debt-to-equity ratio:

$$\text{Debt to Equity} = \frac{\text{Total Debt}}{\text{Total Equity}} \qquad (8.14)$$

The debt-to-equity ratio divides the total debt of the firm by total equity. The debt-to-equity ratio is similar to the debt ratio in Equation 8.13. When the debt ratio is 50 percent (i.e., half of the capital structure of the firm is debt), then the debt-to-equity ratio is 1. While the debt ratio ranges from 0 percent to 100 percent, the debt to equity ranges from zero if a company has no debt (and the numerator is zero) to a very large number up to infinity if equity is at or near zero (and the denominator is at or near zero).

Times interest earned ratio:

$$\text{Times Interest Earned} = \frac{\text{Operating Income}}{\text{Interest Expense}} \qquad (8.15)$$

Operating income is the net income of the firm before interest and taxes. Operating income also excludes income from subsidiaries. Times interest earned equals operating income divided by interest expense.

A company with a high times interest earned ratio is likely to earn enough to pay interest from current period earnings.

Other Ratios or Formulas

Book value (per share) begins with total equity or shareholders' equity. Shareholders' equity includes paid-in common stock, retained earnings, and preferred stock. To calculate the book value of common stock, subtract the value of preferred stock and divide by the number of common shares outstanding.

Book value:

$$\text{Book Value} = \frac{\text{Shareholders' Equity} - \text{Preferred Equity}}{\text{Common Shares Outstanding}} \qquad (8.16)$$

Publicly traded common stock can trade significantly above book value. Book value, however, reflects the cost of the stock in the accounting records.

The price-earnings (P/E) ratio:

$$\text{P/E} = \frac{\text{Market Price per Share}}{\text{EPS}} \qquad (8.17)$$

The P/E ratio divides the prevailing market price of the stock by annual earnings per share. The earnings may be the most recent four quarters of earnings, rather than the most recent calendar year. Other times, people use a forecast of the next four quarters of earnings.

The P/E ratio provides a measure of value. Companies with a high P/E ratio cost more relative to a given amount of earnings as compared to companies with a low P/E ratio. However, companies with high growth potential tend to have higher P/E ratios. The combination of growth and value pricing (i.e., P/E ratio) determine whether a company's shares are an attractive investment.

The dividend yield:

$$\text{Dividend Yield} = \frac{\text{Dividend per Share}}{\text{Market Price per Share}} \qquad (8.18)$$

The dividend yield on a stock equals the annual dividend divided by the market price of the stock. The dividend yield plus gains or losses determine the return to the investor on a common stock.

The payout ratio:

$$\text{Payout Ratio} = \frac{\text{Cash Dividends}}{\text{Net Income}} \qquad (8.19)$$

The payout ratio for a company is the cash dividend divided by net income. The payout ratio equals the percentage of net income actually paid to shareholders.

The payout ratio affects the growth rate of the company. Companies that pay out a higher percentage of net income tend to grow more slowly than companies with low payout ratio. This difference in growth rate occurs because the net income not distributed begins to earn a return, adding to the growth rate for earnings.

TREND ANALYSIS

Analysts review financial results over time. The analysis may involve amounts changes in individual items from the income statement or balance sheet. Analysts are interested in observing the average growth rate over time as well as trends in annual rates of growth.

An important component of any trend analysis is a review of revenues. Analysts may study the growth in unit sales and prices to better understand the reasons for the observed growth in sales revenues. Analysts may look at different business lines or geographic locations to see what factors best explain the recent sales results.

The analyst may calculate the growth rate of expenses such as operating expenses such as COST OF GOODS SOLD, operating expenses, DEPRECIATION, or INTEREST EXPENSE. As a company grows, expenses grow along with sales. Trend analysis of expenses may reveal information about the cost structure (fixed versus variable costs) and sensitivity to commodity prices.

The financial analysis may include a review of the growth rate in various measures of profit such as gross profit; earnings before interest, taxes, depreciation, and amortization (EBITDA); or net income. Faster growth justifies a higher stock price. The growth rate observed may be used as an input into a valuation model.

The analysis may calculate growth rates from the balance sheet, such as total assets, INVENTORY, or RETAINED EARNINGS. Finally, the growth analysis may review financial results appearing on the statement of cash flows such as cash flow from operations, net cash flow, or free cash flow (cash flow from operations adjusted downward by capital investment).

Trends in ratios can reveal important information about a company. The ratios described above provide measures of liquidity, solvency, and profitability. Changes in these ratios can identify problems with a company being able to turn over inventory as rapidly, reflecting the skill of management, the actions of competitors, or indications of product obsolescence. Liquidity ratios and solvency ratios are especially important to lenders, who are primarily interested in the company's ability to repay debt. Investors closely watch changes in profitability because stock prices respond more to changes in profitability than to the absolute level of profits.

INDUSTRY ANALYSIS

Analysts compare the growth rates of companies in the same industry. Companies that excel in marketing, have introduced new products, have made improvements to existing products, or are pricing aggressively may have faster sales growth. Companies that control cost by redesigning products, investing in capital to lower variable costs, outsourcing, or improving manufacturing efficiency should have lower costs and lower growth in costs than peer companies. Companies with greater pricing control due to patent protection, branding, and trademarks may be able to grow profits more rapidly than competitors.

Many of the ratios in this chapter vary significantly from company to company. Analysts compare the ratios of one company to other companies in the same industry. In many cases, companies in the same industry have similar financial ratios, reflecting business conditions in that sector. Companies with higher profitability ratios, higher liquidity ratios, and lower debt tend to enjoy higher stock prices than peer companies that are less profitable, less liquid, or less solvent.

CONCLUSION

Financial statement analysis can review important information about a company by providing a measure of liquidity, profitability, and solvency. Financial statement analysis can identify trends and quantifying growth of key factors of business success. Financial analysis can also compare a company to other companies in the same industry by comparing the financial results, ratios, and growth patterns of the individual companies.

For each of the following financial ratios, determine if you have enough information to calculate the ratio. Then calculate the ratio where possible and comment on conclusions that may be reached about Lavalier Communications, Inc. using this ratio.

8.1. Current ratio

8.2. Acid test or quick ratio

8.3. Accounts receivable turnover

8.4. Days' sales in receivables

8.5. Inventory turnover

8.6. Return on assets

8.7. Return on equity

8.8. Gross profit percentage

8.9. Profit margin

8.10. Asset turnover

8.11. Earnings per share

8.12. Fully diluted EPS

8.13. Debt ratio

8.14. Debt-to-equity ratio

8.15. Times interest earned

8.16. Book value per share

8.17. Price-earnings ratio

8.18. Dividend yield

8.19. Payout ratio

1. You work for Lavalier Corporation. During the past several years, you have been working with the company to develop new communication technologies. Based primarily on your efforts, the company has acquired several valuable patents. The company has decided that the most attractive way of commercializing these patents is to set up a new company and provide you with a substantial equity stake in the business. Lavalier company lawyers have created a U.S. "C" corporation (the standard U.S. corporate structure) named Lavalier Communications, Inc.(LCI). Late in 20X0, the new company created a board of directors from senior officers in Lavalier Corporation and several independent (outside) directors. On January 2, 20X1, the board of directors met and named you president and chief operating officer (COO) of the new company. The board also named the corporate treasurer of Lavalier Corporation as the chairman and chief executive officer (CEO). The board of directors authorized 5 million shares of common stock ($1 par value). On January 2, 20X1, Lavalier transferred $5 million to a newly established bank account at First National Bank in return for 1 million shares of common stock (par value $1 per share).

2. On January 2, 20X1, the board of LCI also granted you options to buy 200,000 shares of stock at $5 per share expiring in 5 years. The options may be exercised (i.e., you can exchange the options plus $5 per share of common stock) at any point after 3 years up to expiration in five years.

3. Based on prior discussions, the bank immediately moved $2 million into a 5 percent bond maturing 12/31/X3. The remaining funds remain in a demand deposit account earning a floating rate of interest.

4. On January 2, 20X1, as agreed in the December Lavalier Corporation board meeting, LCI acquires key patents from Lavalier Bermuda PLC for $2 million.

5. On January 4, you hire four employees (including yourself) for salaries totaling $600,000 per year, payable monthly. However, 20 percent of the salaries are withheld for payroll taxes.

6. On each quarter end (March 31, June 30, September 30, and December 31), the company files payroll tax forms and pays the withheld taxes to the federal government (for simplicity, assume there is no state tax or company portion of payroll taxes). (Posting only March 31 entries)

7. On January 16, you lease office space for three years at a nearby office park for $4,000 per month beginning in February. On January 16, you make a security deposit of one month's rent and pay the first month's rent. Additional rent payments are due on the first day of each month beginning March 1. (Show entries through March.)

8. On January 19, you buy miscellaneous office equipment totaling $45,000. Your auditing firm advises you to use a 4-year life, zero residual value and suggests you use the straight-line method of depreciation. Your auditor believes it is acceptable to treat the current year as a full year for depreciation purposes. Your vendor expects payment in 45 days to avoid finance charges of 1¼% per month, so you pay on 2/27/X1.

9. On January 28, you contract with a multinational custom manufacturer to produce 10,000 new communication devices (NCDs) per month. They will ship you 5,000 in June, then 10,000 per month after that for a net (delivered) price of $10 per unit. The manufacturer asks you to make a one-time advance payment for the first three months' supply to provide them with part of the funding for setting up the new manufacturing process.

10. You decide to lease additional patents from the company. On March 31, you make the first quarterly payment of $30,000 to license additional patents from Lavalier Bermuda PLC.

11. You receive 5,000 NCDs on June 19.

12. You ship 3,500 NCDs on June 22 to OEM Communications for a gross price of $26 per unit to be paid within 30 days. A commission of 20 percent is payable to Lavalier Sales and Marketing (Channel Islands). Based on the prior experience of Lavalier Corporation, you predict that 3 percent of sales is uncollectible.

13. On June 30, you receive semiannual interest on the bond. You do not reinvest the interest from the June 30 payment in any investment.

14. You receive payment in full on July 18 for the June sales to OEM Communications. You pay the sales commission to Lavalier Sales and Marketing (Channel Islands) and keep the balance of the cash in your demand deposit account.

15. You receive 10,000 NCDs on July 23.

16. You sell 9,500 NCDs on July 25 to Excellent Acoustics for $25.75 against a cash payment in full. Lavalier Sales and Marketing (Channel Islands) was not involved in the transaction, so no commission is payable. Despite the advance payment, you decide to expense for uncollectibles anyway.

17. You receive 10,000 NCDs on August 22.

18. You sell 11,000 NCDs on August 26 to Acme Electronics for $26.25 for payment in 30 days. Lavalier Sales and Marketing (Channel Islands) was not involved in the transaction, so no commission is payable. You maintain a 3 percent allowance for uncollectibles.

19. You receive 10,000 NCDs on September 19. You pay the contract manufacturer seven days later.

20. You ship 9,500 NCDs on September 22 to OEM Communications for a gross price of $27.50 per unit to be paid within 30 days. A commission of 20 percent is payable to Lavalier Sales and Marketing (Channel Islands). Based on the prior experience of Lavalier Corporation, you predict that 3 percent of the sale is uncollectible.

21. You learn that Acme Electronics is in financial trouble. Acme asks you for relief on the payment of $288,750. You agree to accept $242,000, which arrives on 10/15/X1.

22. You receive payment from OEM Communications for the September 22 sale.

23. You receive 10,000 NCDs on October 22. You pay the invoice amount (at $10/unit) immediately.

24. You sell 10,000 NCDs on October 25 to Excellent Acoustics for $26 against a cash payment in full. Lavalier Sales and Marketing (Channel Islands) was not involved in the transaction, so no commission is payable. Despite the advance payment, you decide to expense for uncollectibles anyway. You decide to reserve 4 percent of sales as uncollectible from now on.

25. You receive 10,000 NCDs on November 21. You pay the invoice amount (at $10/unit) immediately.

26. You sell 10,000 NCDs on November 25 to Excellent Acoustics for $26 against a cash payment in full. Lavalier Sales and Marketing (Channel Islands) was not involved in the transaction, so no commission is payable. Despite the advance payment, you decide to expense for uncollectibles anyway. You decide to reserve 4 percent of sales as uncollectible from now on.

27. You receive 10,000 NCDs on December 21. You pay the invoice amount (at $10/unit) January 11, 20X0.

28. You sell 11,000 NCDs on December 28 to Zebutronics Communications for $26.50 with payment due in 30 days. No commission is payable.

29. On December 31, you receive the semiannual interest payment on the bond investment. You do not reinvest the interest from the December 31 payment in a new investment.

30. To complete the year, you calculate the amortization on the patents acquired on January 19 for $2 million. You decide that the patents had 10 years of useful life remaining when acquired.

31. Oops. Although you received monthly statements from the bank, you realize you haven't booked the interest income totaling $31,125.66. You discuss the matter with your auditor, who suggests you enter the total in one entry on 12/31/20X1 since you haven't closed the books yet.

CHAPTER 1

1.1. You work for Lavalier Corporation. During the past several years, you have been working with the company to develop new communication technologies. Based primarily on your efforts, the company has acquired several valuable patents. The company has decided that the most attractive way of commercializing these patents is to set up a new company and provide you with a substantial equity stake in the business. Lavalier company lawyers have created a U.S. "C" corporation (the standard U.S. corporate structure) named Lavalier Communications, Inc. (LCI). Late in 20X0, the new company created a board of directors from senior officers in Lavalier Corporation and several independent (outside) directors. On January 2, 20X1, the board of directors met and named you president and chief operating officer (COO) of the new company. The board also named the corporate treasurer of Lavalier Corporation as the chairman and chief executive officer (CEO). The board of directors authorized 5 million shares of common stock ($1 par value). On January 2, 20X1, Lavalier transferred $5 million to a newly established bank account at First National Bank in return for 1 million shares of common stock (par value $1 per share).

01/02/X1	CASH	$5,000,000	
01/02/X1	COMMON STOCK		$1,000,000
01/02/X1	PAID-IN CAPITAL IN EXCESS OF PAR		$4,000,000

The debit entry for cash follows the most basic rule of double-entry accounting. Cash is an asset, and the cash received from Lavalier Corporation is the first asset owned by the new company LCI. Companies usually have more than one bank account, and the name of the asset does not suggest a particular bank account. LCI would establish a separate asset account or subaccount for each account so that the accounting records can reflect the cash balances in each bank account. For some types of assets, it is common to not create a large number of accounts but instead keep track of such details separately.

The credit entry to common stock for $1 million may not be obvious. The entry is a credit because increases to capital are entered as credits. But it is tempting to enter the entire $5 million as COMMON STOCK, reflecting the historical cost of the transaction. In most cases, accountants use transaction prices to determine the cost of items in the accounting records. The credits above do follow that convention, except that the historical cost is divided between two equity accounts.

The question stated that the common stock was created with a par value of $1 per share. Here, the entries reflect that par amount (1 million shares at $1 per share). The additional amount of $4 per share above the $1 par is carried in another account usually titled something like "ADDITIONAL PAID-IN CAPITAL IN EXCESS OF PAR." The capital was created by an investment in LCI, not from profits. Accountants preserve that detail by accounting for profits held as capital in another equity account introduced later called RETAINED EARNINGS.

Accounting records do not reflect the 5 million shares authorized by the company. LCI has been granted permission to issue 5 million shares but has issued only 1 million. Having the authority to sell additional shares permits the company to raise capital from new investors, including venture capitalists and employees, and through a public offering. The company can also grant shares or options to buy shares to employees as incentive compensation.

1.2. On January 2, 20X1, the board of LCI also granted you options to buy 200,000 shares of stock at $5 per share expiring in five years. The options may be exercised (i.e., you can exchange the options plus $5 per share of common stock) at any point after three years up to expiration in five years.

No entries are required at this time.

This is clearly a "trick" question because it requires the reader to know some particular details about how accountants handle certain types of transactions. The purpose of the question is to introduce the ideas outside of the chapter, so that students are free to explore the ideas in more detail.

Accountants could record the fair value of the options, but they are not required to record anything in this case. Most companies in this situation choose to enter nothing and even design their option awards so that they can enter nothing.

If the price you had to pay on exercise (the strike price) was below the value of the stock on the day the option was awarded, the company would have to enter that difference as a debit to an equity account (probably in an account labeled EMPLOYEE STOCK OPTIONS or OPTIONS GRANTED UNDER LONG-TERM INCENTIVE PLAN.

Current accounting rules also require LCI to value and disclose the value of these options in the footnotes of the financial statements. The value would reflect the updated price of LCI common shares, the remaining time until expiration, and other market inputs, including interest rates and volatility. This text will not discuss these inputs or the valuation methods. Further, these footnoted valuations will not affect the financial statements.

Had the board of LCI granted shares of common stock instead of options, the accountants would need to decide how to handle the grant. The company may be able to avoid any accounting of the grant by not delivering shares but instead promising to do so at a future time contingent on results or other milestones.

If LCI granted shares at the time the company was organized, the accountants would probably value the grant at the same $5 per share that the company paid. This value would add to the amount of capital the company shows in its accounting records at $5 per share for the total shares granted (a credit entry). The offsetting debit would be an asset. Probably, the accountants would use an asset account like ORGANIZATIONAL COSTS. This asset would reflect the future benefit the company would gain from those receiving grants of stock. Chapter 5 describes how these assets can affect how and when items are recognized as expenses by the company.

The existence of organizational costs can affect all the financial statements of the company. Of course, the balance sheet would immediately show more capital and assets. Accounting rules require that these organizational assets be removed from the balance sheet quickly (currently in one year). As the assets are removed, the net income will be reduced by the amount of the organizational costs. As a result, the grant can affect the company's income statement, the balance sheet, and a variety of financial ratios.

1.3. Based on prior discussions, the bank immediately moved $2 million into a 5 percent bond maturing 12/31/X3. The remaining funds remain in a demand deposit account earning a floating rate of interest.

| 01/02/X1 | Investment in Bonds | $2,000,000 | |
| 01/02/X1 | Cash | | $2,000,000 |

Of course, cash goes down by $2 million, which accountants represent as a credit of $2 million. Earlier, the accountants posted a debit to CASH for $5 million. After the withdrawal in Question 1.3, the account will carry $3 million (the net of debits less credits to CASH).

The cash, an asset, is exchanged for another asset, the bonds. To show an increase in this new investment, accountants post a debit to a new account. Because this bond matures more than one year in the future, accountants need to use an investment account that reflects the longer life of that asset. This asset will be a long-term asset. Chapter 3 will show how different types of assets are classified on the balance sheet. Chapter 8 (Financial Statement Analysis) will explore how that classification can be used to analyze a company's financial position.

1.4. On January 2, 20X1, as agreed in the December Lavalier Corporation board meeting, LCI acquires key patents from Lavalier Bermuda PLC for $2 million.

| 01/02/01 | PATENTS | $2,000,000 | |
| 01/02/01 | CASH | | $2,000,000 |

As above, $2 million is withdrawn from the bank and accountants reflect this transaction, just as in Question 1.3, as credit to CASH. The CASH account has now received a debit (increase) of $5 million and two credits (decreases) of $2 million each. Accountants net the debits and credits ($5 million – $2 million – $2 million) and can determine that the company now carries $1 million in the bank account.

As in Question 1.3, a new asset account called PATENTS is created. The accountants accept that the $2 million paid for the patents is the best measure of the value to use on the financial statements, so they debit the account for $2 million.

Patents don't last forever and may lose their value before the company loses their legal rights. LCI must account for the loss in value over time, but this will appear as a question in a later chapter.

There is reason to question the $2 million valuation. Faced with internal transfers, prices may not reflect fair value. Lavalier Bermuda PLC appears to be another subsidiary of Lavalier Corporation. Bermuda has favorable tax treatment. Likewise, the $2 million paid for the patents can become a deductible cost on the U.S. corporate income tax return for LCI. The companies involved may need to establish that $2 million is a fair value both to outside auditors and to tax authorities.

Note that the description in Question 1.1 suggests that these are internally developed patents and, in general, a company cannot include the cost of developing patents on their balance sheet. However, the out-of-pocket costs paid by Lavalier Corporation are deductions that lower taxable income. If LCI had bought the patents from Lavalier Corporation, the corporation would have a taxable gain. All this suggests that the Lavalier Corporation is aware of tax considerations, but it is not apparent that LCI is doing anything wrong as long as accountants can establish that the transfer occurred at fair market value.

1.5. On January 16, you lease office space for one year at a nearby office park for $4,000 per month beginning in February. On January 16, you make a security deposit of one month's rent and pay the first month's rent. Additional rent payments are due on the first day of each month beginning March 1. Show entries through March.

1/16/20X1	SECURITY DEPOSIT	$4,000	
1/16/20X1	PREPAID RENT	$4,000	
1/16/20X1	CASH		$8,000

Question 1.5 shows another withdrawal of cash, in this case, to make payments to a new landlord. The withdrawal shows up again as a credit to cash. The cash balance will be reduced again, reflected in the net of the initial debit of $5 million and all of the credits in the account.

Part of the payment is a security deposit that the landlord will hold during the lease. This deposit could be used at some future time to pay for damages to the property or to offset unpaid rent. Or, if there are no charges for damages and if LCI pays all the future rents, they can expect to receive the deposit back. In all cases, the deposit represents future benefits to the company, so it is an asset. The entry to the SECURITY DEPOSIT asset account is a debit, which is how we have been increasing the value of all other asset accounts so far.

Because these transactions are posted on January 16, it is too early to reflect the rental charges in the company accounts. The account called PREPAID RENT is not an expense (at least not yet). Chapter 4 introduces the idea of expenses, and accountants will at that point create an expense account to handle the rent transactions. As mentioned above, Chapter 5 will explain other ways that asset accounts can be used to affect the timing of accounting transactions in the financial statements.

1.6. On January 19, you buy miscellaneous office equipment totaling $45,000. Your vendor expects payment in 45 days to avoid finance charges of 1 percent per month so you pay on 2/27/X9.

1/19/20X1	EQUIPMENT	$45,000	
1/19/20X1	ACCOUNTS PAYABLE		$45,000
2/27/20X1	ACCOUNTS PAYABLE	$45,000	
2/27/20X1	CASH		$45,000

As before, accountants use a new account. In this case, the asset EQUIPMENT is used to account for the office equipment. As with all assets, the value of the equipment purchased shows up as a debit to EQUIPMENT, reflecting the increase in value for this asset. The value used for the asset is the value paid to the merchant for the equipment. This arm's-length price or historical cost is an objective measure of value.

Unlike previous examples, LCI did not immediately pay for the equipment. Instead, the company incurred a liability or future obligation. This trade credit is posted to an account called ACCOUNTS PAYABLE. The value used for the liability is also the value paid to the merchant for the equipment. As a result, the debit and the credit match.

When LCI pays for the equipment on February 27, cash declines by $45,000. The cash payment is again posted as a credit, and the CASH account will reflect the updated cash balance on February 27. Until then, the cash balance will not show the $45,000 decline. In particular, the balance sheet at month-end (January 31) will show the higher cash balance and a liability of $45,000.

Also on February 27, the liability is repaid. To reduce the balance in ACCOUNTS PAYABLE by $45,000, accountants debit the account. After the payment has been posted, the ACCOUNTS PAYABLE account reflects a credit of $45,000 offset by a $45,000 debit. The account now shows a zero balance on the accounting records.

To recap, assets go up on January 19, when the EQUIPMENT account first reflects the new equipment. At the same time, a new liability account also goes up. In this way, the purchase of the equipment does not affect the equity of the company. Then on February 19, the liability is repaid, but another asset—cash—declines by a like amount. On February 27, the equity of the company remains unchanged.

Equipment does not last forever, and the company will need to reflect this wear and tear in the accounting records. Questions following Chapter 5 will show how accountants handle the use of the equipment over time.

1.7. On January 28, you contract with a multinational custom manufacturer to produce 10,000 New Communication Devices (NCDs) per month. They will ship you 5,000 in June, then 10,000 per month after that, for a net delivered price of $10 per unit. The manufacturer asks you to make a one-time advance payment for the first three months' supply to provide them with part of the funding for setting up the new manufacturing process.

1/28/20X1	ADVANCES TO SUPPLIERS	$250,000
1/28/20X1	CASH	$250,000

The transactions follow a familiar pattern. In this case, yet another asset account is used to reflect the future value of inventory the company will eventually receive. LCI is paying for 25,000 units (5,000 in the first month, then 10,000 per month) at $10 in advance. This type of trade financing is common in some industries. To increase the balance in the ADVANCES TO SUPPLIERS account, accountants debit the account for an amount equal to the amount advanced to the supplier.

It would be possible to use an account called INVENTORY as the asset account to record this transaction. The company has not yet used an INVENTORY account but it will shortly, and the account could be used to reflect inventory that the company has paid for but not received. However, the advanced payment is more of a financing trade than purchase of goods at this point. The risks to LCI are different than the risks of holding delivered inventory. Further, if LCI accounts for the future value as inventory, then accounting records would not be able to reflect the eventual receipt of physical inventory.

The credit to CASH follows the preceding pattern. A credit equal to $250,000 updates the CASH account to the new cash balance. As before, the exchange of one asset (cash) for another asset (viewed as either a loan to suppliers or inventory) does not affect the equity of LCI.

1.8. You receive 5,000 NCDs on June 19.

6/19/20X1	INVENTORY	$50,000
6/19/20X1	ADVANCES TO SUPPLIERS	$50,000

If the company instead debited INVENTORY in Question 1.7, accountants would need to make no entry at this time. If LCI created an account reflecting the advance to suppliers, then it would be necessary to reflect the receipt of the first shipment of inventory.

The debit puts the value of the 5,000 units (at $10 each) into the new asset account INVENTORY. As the accountants have done before, the value of the inventory is the actual amount paid for the inventory.

The credit to ADVANCES TO SUPPLIERS reduces the amount held in that asset account. The reduction to this account reflects that the supplier has satisfied part of its obligation and LCI now carries some inventory and a reduced amount for future benefits (i.e., the merchandise they expect to receive).

1.9. You receive 10,000 NCDs on July 23. Question 1.9 follows the pattern in Question 1.8 but reflects the value of 10,000 units instead of 5,000.

7/23/20X1	Finished Goods Inventory	$100,000	
7/23/20X1	Advances to suppliers		$100,000

1.10. You receive 10,000 NCDs on August 22. Question 1.10 follows the pattern in Questions 1.8 and 1.9.

1.11. You receive 10,000 NCDs on September 19. You pay the contract manufacturer seven days later.

9/19/20X1	Finished Goods Inventory	$100,000	
9/19/20X1	Accounts Payable		$100,000
9/26/20X1	Accounts Payable	$100,000	
9/26/20X1	Cash		$100,000

Now that the manufacturer has shipped 25,000 units, LCI must pay for inventory it receives. The transactions between LCI and the contract manufacturer now follow a common pattern. LCI receives 10,000 units of inventory on September 19 and debits the asset INVENTORY to reflect that receipt. Because the company does not immediately pay the invoice, the accountants credit a liability for $100,000, equal to the value of the inventory in the company accounts. On September 19, an increase to an asset is matched with an equal increase of a liability.

On September 26, the company pays the invoice. To show the decrease in the liability, accountants debit ACCOUNTS PAYABLE. The credit to CASH reduces an asset. Because of the credit and subsequent debit to ACCOUNTS PAYABLE, accountants can reflect the one-week difference between the receipt of the goods and payment.

1.12. You receive 10,000 NCDs on October 22. You pay the invoice amount (at $10/unit) immediately.

10/22/20X1	Finished Goods Inventory	$100,000	
10/22/20X1	Cash		$100,000

   This pattern may not be typical of corporate buying and remittance but it simplifies the accounting entries for this question and answer. These entries are included so that there are a complete set of debits and credits to use later for preparing financial statements for the year.

1.13. You receive 10,000 NCDs on November 21. You pay the invoice amount (at $10/unit) immediately. Same as Question 1.12.

11/21/20X1	Finished Goods Inventory	$100,000	
11/21/20X1	Cash		$100,000

1.14. You receive 10,000 NCDs on December 21. You pay the invoice amount (at $10/unit) immediately. Same as Questions 1.12 and 1.13.

11/21/20X1	Finished Goods Inventory	$100,000	
11/21/20X1	Cash		$100,000

CHAPTER 2

2.1. By the end of the first quarter, March 31, 20X1, LCI has no sales or even any saleable inventory. Shares of similar publicly traded technology companies sell for less than book value. Should LCI write down their equity on indications that it is worth less than $5 per share?
   Currently, the book value of the liabilities and equity equal the book value of LCI assets. The accounting records are based on historical cost. The individual assets may become worth more or less over time, but accountants in general do not adjust the value, so there is no reason to adjust the value of equity.
   In fact, book value and market value can differ significantly, and the size of the difference is not a factor in the decision on how to value items on the balance sheet.
   A company that acquires assets, especially custom-built equipment, may never be able to resell the assets at the price paid. Just like a new car, these assets may lose market value. But accountants of going concerns will generally leave values at historical cost.

Accounting records contain some assets that are not necessarily carried at book value. For example, goodwill (usually created when one company pays more than book value to buy another company) remains at historical cost. But companies must regularly review goodwill to determine whether the value has decreased. Other assets, such as equipment, are reduced by depreciation. Likewise, natural resources are reduced by depletion, and intangible assets are reduced by amortization. Chapter 5 explains the ways these assets are revalued.

2.2. Suppose LCI pays $10 per unit to suppliers to buy 5,000 units of inventory on 6/19/20X1 and sells 3,500 units at $26 on 6/22/20X1. Has the company violated the matching principle because the dollar amount of the sales ($26 × 3,500 = $91,000) and the costs ($10 × 5,000 = $50,000) do not match, the dates of the entries do not match, and the number of units does not match?

The idea of matching applies to revenues and expenses, which will be introduced in Chapters 4 and 5. The idea of matching will be clear once the student has reviewed these chapters. For the time being, a clarification may help the reader understand the way accountants would account for the purchase of inventory and the sale of those goods to customers.

Double-entry accounting requires debits and equal credits to be posted together, but accountants would not pair this sale with this purchase of inventory. These amounts should not be equal in most cases, and, generally, companies buy inventory before they sell it. The difference contributes to profitability.

When the company buys the inventory, the cash payment equals the value of the newly acquired inventory. INVENTORY is debited for $50,000, and CASH (or perhaps ACCOUNTS PAYABLE) is credited an equal amount on 6/19/20X1. Chapter 4 will show how the sales are booked when revenue accounts are introduced. Accountants will post a debit to cash equal to $91,000 and a credit to a revenue account on June 22.

The timing of the purchase of the inventory and the sale of the inventory is just three days apart, but the difference could be much longer. The idea of matching is that the company carries the $50,000 paid for inventory as an asset until the goods are sold. Chapter 4 will demonstrate how the sale of inventory is finally recognized as a cost. Accountants seek to match the timing of the revenues generated and the costs incurred, and use a variety of techniques introduced in Chapters 4 and 5.

CHAPTER 3

3.1. Following is a list of all the balance sheet accounts that have been used in the Questions in this book. Next to each account is the sum of all the debits to that account and the sum of all credits to that account. Note that these totals reflect all the debits and credits to each account in all chapters of the text, not just the previous two chapters. Use the information to construct a balance sheet for LCI.

Account	Debit	Credit
CASH	$6,490,001	$5,433,450
SECURITY DEPOSITS	4,000	0
ADVANCES TO SUPPLIERS	250,000	250,000
ACCOUNTS RECEIVABLE	932,500	641,000
ALLOWANCE FOR UNCOLLECTIBLES	25,564	59,029
FINISHED GOODS INVENTORY	650,000	645,000
PREPAID RENT	4,000	4,000
INVESTMENT IN BONDS	2,000,000	0
EQUIPMENT	45,000	0
ACCUMULATED DEPRECIATION	0	11,250
PATENTS	2,000,000	200,000
ACCOUNTS PAYABLE	215,450	315,450
PAYROLL TAXES PAYABLE	120,000	120,000
COMMON STOCK	0	1,000,000
PAID-IN CAPITAL IN EXCESS OF PAR	$ 0	$4,000,000

Balance Sheet for Lavalier Communications, Inc. for the Year Ending 12/31/20X1

Short-Term Assets		
CASH	$1,056,551	
SECURITY DEPOSITS	4,000	
ADVANCES TO SUPPLIERS	0	
ACCOUNTS RECEIVABLE	291,500	
ALLOWANCE FOR UNCOLLECTIBLE ACCOUNTS	(33,465)	258,035
FINISHED GOODS INVENTORY	5,000	
PREPAID RENT	0	
TOTAL SHORT-TERM ASSETS	1,323,586	

(Continued)

Long-Term Assets

INVESTMENT IN BONDS	2,000,000	
EQUIPMENT	45,000	
ACCUMULATED DEPRECIATION	(11,250)	33,750
PATENTS	1,800,000	
TOTAL LONG-TERM ASSETS	3,833,750	
TOTAL ASSETS	5,157,336	

Liabilities

ACCOUNTS PAYABLE	100,000
PAYROLL TAXES PAYABLE	0
TOTAL LIABILITIES	100,000

Equity

RETAINED EARNINGS	57,336
COMMON STOCK	1,000,000
PAID-IN CAPITAL IN EXCESS OF PAR	4,000,000
TOTAL EQUITY	5,057,336
TOTAL LIABILITIES AND EQUITY	$5,157,336

To construct the balance sheet, net the total debits against the total credits for all the balance sheet accounts. For assets, use total debits less total credits. For contra-assets, liabilities, and equity, use total credits less total debits.

CHAPTER 4

4.1. Rent payments are due on the first day of each month beginning February 1. Show entries through year-end.

2/1/20X1	RENT EXPENSE	$4,000	
2/1/20X1	PREPAID RENT		4,000
3/1/20X1	RENT EXPENSE	4,000	
3/1/20X1	CASH		4,000
4/1/20X1	RENT EXPENSE	4,000	
4/1/20X1	CASH		4,000
5/1/20X1	RENT EXPENSE	4,000	
5/1/20X1	CASH		4,000
6/1/20X1	RENT EXPENSE	4,000	
6/1/20X1	CASH		4,000
7/1/20X1	RENT EXPENSE	4,000	

7/1/20X1	CASH		4,000
8/1/20X1	RENT EXPENSE	4,000	
8/1/20X1	CASH		4,000
9/1/20X1	RENT EXPENSE	4,000	
9/1/20X1	CASH		4,000
10/1/20X1	RENT EXPENSE	4,000	
10/1/20X1	CASH		4,000
11/1/20X1	RENT EXPENSE	4,000	
11/1/20X1	CASH		4,000
12/1/20X1	RENT EXPENSE	4,000	
12/1/20X1	CASH		$4,000

The rent expense appears as a debit. The rent expense each month is always posted as a debit. As explained in Chapter 4, this expense, along with all revenues and expenses for the company are temporary accounts. Therefore, the impact of the monthly $4,000 expenses is to reduce net income. Eventually, the net income or loss will be added to LCI equity as retained earnings.

The offsetting credit in February is the asset account PREPAID RENT. Recall from Chapter 1 (Question 1.5) that the landlord asked for a security deposit plus the first month's rent, which LCI paid on January 16. However, the company did not recognize the February expense at that time. Instead, the accountants created an asset account called PREPAID RENT to postpone the timing of the rent expense.

Beginning in March, LCI must pay for rent with additional cash payments. The expense is posted as a debit to the RENT EXPENSE account and the credit to CASH accounts for the payment of cash to the landlord and the reduction in cash held in the bank.

Notice that all the rent expenditures appear in a list together and not in chronological order with the rest of the company's entries. In all the previous examples, we created debits and credits when we learned about a business transaction. It is possible to create the entries well in advance of the actual rent payment because the date at the beginning of the record identifies when the debit and credit should be reflected in the accounting records. Likewise, the system that transforms a series of debits and credits into financial statements must be able to discern which entries to include and which to exclude, based on the date of the business transaction.

4.2. You decide to lease additional patents from the company. On March 31, you make the first quarterly payment of $30,000 to license additional patents from Lavalier Bermuda PLC.

3/31/20X1	PATENT LICENSE EXPENSE	$30,000	
3/31/20X1	CASH		30,000
6/30/20X1	PATENT LICENSE EXPENSE	30,000	
6/30/20X1	CASH		30,000
9/30/20X1	PATENT LICENSE EXPENSE	30,000	
9/30/20X1	CASH		30,000
12/31/20X1	PATENT LICENSE EXPENSE	30,000	
12/31/20X1	CASH		$30,000

In Chapter 1 (Question 1.4), LCI bought patents. In this case, LCI is paying a periodic payment for the right (not necessarily the exclusive right) to use other patents. Accountants handle these royalty payments just like other expenses. Each payment appears as a debit matched with a credit equal to the amount of cash payment.

4.3. You ship 3,500 NCDs on June 22 to OEM Communications for a gross price of $26 per unit to be paid within 30 days.

6/22/20X1	ACCOUNTS RECEIVABLE	$91,000	
6/22/20X1	SALES REVENUE		91,000
6/22/20X1	COST OF GOODS SOLD	35,000	
6/22/20X1	FINISHED GOODS INVENTORY		$35,000

The heart of the transaction is a sale of 3,500 units times the price of $26, which produces sales revenue of $91,000 paid for inventory costing $35,000 (3,500 units at $10 each). Although the sale and the reduction in inventory are tied together, it is clear from the list of accounting entries that double-entry accounting involves more than this link in actions.

The SALES REVENUE account is a temporary account that represents a direct contribution to net income and eventually equity through retained earnings. As with all revenues, accountants record sales as a credit. If the customer paid cash, this transaction would resemble the myrrh trades described in Chapter 1 with a debit to cash. Instead, the company creates another asset called ACCOUNTS RECEIVABLE that equals the value of the sale. Once again, accountants have used historical cost (the transaction price) as the basis for valuation in the income statement.

The company gives up inventory as part of the transaction. The quantity of goods decreases by 3,500, so the value of the remaining inventory declines by $35,000. Accountants record this decrease in value to an asset as a credit to the asset holding the inventory value.

Recall that the inventory account was used to postpone recognizing the $10 per unit paid to acquire the product. It is now time to recognize the expense and the account used to put product cost into the income statement is COST OF GOODS. Accountants debit the COST OF GOODS account using the historical price (in this case $10 per unit).

The net impact of the trade is a decrease in one asset (INVENTORY) by $35,000 and an increase in another asset (ACCOUNTS RECEIVABLE) by $91,000. Just like the myrrh trader, LCI has benefited by the sale by the amount that $91,000 exceeds $35,000.

Note that accountants don't net the two values to calculate the profit on the exchange. Instead, they create journal entries much like the ancient system of urns and pebbles. They can, however, see how the company is doing by reviewing the urns. Because these accounts are temporary accounts, the amount accumulated in SALES and COST OF GOODS SOLD represent a running total of these revenues and expenses. Because the accounts start at zero at the beginning of each accounting period, accountants can determine profitability not of a particular exchange but of all exchanges to date.

4.4. On June 30, you receive semiannual interest on the bond. You leave the June 30 payment in your bank account.

6/30/20X1	CASH	$50,000	
6/30/20X1	INTEREST REVENUE		$50,000

Accountants create a new account called INTEREST REVENUE. Like all revenues, accountants post a credit to enter the revenue into the accounting system. The offsetting entry is CASH, which requires a debit to reflect the receipt of $50,000 as interest.

4.5. You receive payment in full on July 18 for the June sales to OEM Communications.

7/18/20X1	CASH	$91,000	
7/18/20X1	ACCOUNTS RECEIVABLE		$91,000

The company receives full payment for the June 22 sale. Accountants debit CASH to reflect the receipt of $91,000. Accountants credit the ACCOUNTS RECEIVABLE account to reflect that LCI no longer has an asset representing the future receipt of cash.

4.6. Oops. It is early January 20X2. Although LCI received monthly statements from the bank, they haven't booked the interest income totaling $31,125.66 for 20X1. LCI accountants discuss the matter with LCI's auditor, who suggests they enter the total in one entry on 12/31/20X1 since LCI has not closed the books yet.

12/31/20X1	CASH	$31,126	
12/31/20X1	INTEREST REVENUE		$31,126

The debits and credits appear as expected and follow the pattern for the interest received on June 30. The cash received appears as a debit for the amount of the money deposited. The revenue appears as a credit and will appear on the income statement for 20X1.

LCI should have been entering interest revenue each month when the company received each bank statement. However, companies make mistakes in creating their financial records. The company, together with LCI's independent auditor, concludes that a single correcting entry is sufficient.

LCI could still post the monthly income as 12 pairs of debits and credits. The company could rerun monthly and quarterly financial statements reflecting the correction. However, LCI has no lenders or other investors to see the corrected interim statements. Lavalier Corporation probably consolidates LCI results into the parent's financial statements, but Lavalier Corporation's quarterly statements are most likely unaudited. Further, the amount of interest omitted from the LCI income statement in prior quarters may be small enough that company auditors determine that the amount is not material on Lavalier Corporation returns.

4.7. Following is a list of all the income statement accounts that have been used in the questions in this book. Next to each account is the sum of all the debits to that account and the sum of all credits to that account. Note that these totals reflect all the debits and credits to each account in all chapters of the text, not just the previous three chapters. Use the information to construct an income statement.

Revenues

SALES REVENUE	$1,697,125	
INTEREST REVENUE	131,126	
TOTAL REVENUES		1,828,251

Expenses

COST OF GOODS SOLD	645,000
SALARY EXPENSE	480,000
COMMISSION EXPENSE	70,450
PAYROLL TAX EXPENSE	120,000
RENT EXPENSE	44,000
UNCOLLECTIBLE	80,215
ACCOUNT EXPENSE	
DEPRECIATION	11,250
EXPENSE—EQUIPMENT	
AMORTIZATION	200,000
EXPENSE—PATENTS	
PATENT LICENSE EXPENSE	120,000

TOTAL EXPENSES	1,770,915
NET INCOME	$57,336

CHAPTER 5

5.1. Revisit the June 22 transaction described in Question 4.3. Now, two additional provisions have been added—a commission and an allowance for nonpayment. You ship 3,500 NCDs on June 22 to OEM Communications for a gross price of $26 per unit to be paid within 30 days. A commission of 20 percent is payable to Lavalier Sales and Marketing (Channel Islands). Based on the prior experience of Lavalier Corporation, you predict that 3 percent of sales will be uncollectible.

6/22/20X1	ACCOUNTS RECEIVABLE	$91,000	
6/22/20X1	SALES REVENUE		91,000
6/22/20X1	COST OF GOODS SOLD	35,000	
6/22/20X1	FINISHED GOODS INVENTORY		35,000
6/22/20X1	COMMISSION EXPENSE	18,200	
6/22/20X1	ACCOUNTS PAYABLE		18,200
6/22/20X1	UNCOLLECTIBLE EXPENSE	2,730	
6/22/20X1	ALLOWANCE FOR UNCOLLECTIBLES		$2,730

One transaction has led to eight accounting entries in LCI's books. The first four entries repeat the answer to Question 4.3. Now we see that the company has a couple of additional costs. The first cost is a commission payable to another part of the company called Lavalier Sales and Marketing (Channel Islands). The accountants don't know much about the terms of this marketing agreement, but the expense of $18,200 is real. Accountants handle this expense like others—as a debit. The sale creates an obligation to pay the same amount, which they handle as an increase to a liability account called ACCOUNTS PAYABLE.

The way the accountants have booked the commission expense represents that LCI has an obligation to pay the commission to the marketing subsidiary even if OEM Communications fails to pay for the goods they received. If the commission is not payable if the company cannot collect, then the accountants would need to record the transactions differently, reflecting the contingent nature of the expense.

The second expense is an accrued expense to recognize the cost of losses on credit sales. LCI expects that some customers will not pay for credit sales and uses an estimate of 3 percent of all sales. Companies often use this method, sometimes applying the percentage only to sales made on credit.

LCI doesn't know which sales are going to become uncollectible. Of course, if they knew that a potential customer was not going to be able to pay the invoice cost of the sale, they would not make the sale. At the same time, LCI recognizes that some sales will become uncollectible.

LCI recognizes the $2,730 expense as a way of adjusting downward the profitability of this sale and all sales. By recognizing the expense at the time of the sale, LCI is accelerating the timing of the expense and is matching the recognition of the expense to the recognition of the sales revenue.

The UNCOLLECTIBLE EXPENSE is booked as a debit, just like other expenses. However, the expense represents a credit loss that has not yet occurred. The accountants need an account to credit, but it does not make sense to use a liability. Nothing about the account resembles a liability because the $2,730 doesn't create any future obligation. The missing account is also not an equity account. The UNCOLLECTIBLE EXPENSE already represents a reduction in equity (when the temporary account is closed out to RETAINED EARNINGS), so it makes no sense to also credit an equity account.

The credit above is to an account called ALLOWANCE FOR UNCOLLECTIBLES. This account is a contra-asset account. This account acts to reduce the value of the ACCOUNTS RECEIVABLE account. Taken together, the amount the company expects to receive is $91,000 (the amount the customer has committed to pay) less $2,730, the allowance amount reflecting adjustments for future credit losses.

Later, when the company experiences a credit loss, accountants will reduce the ACCOUNTS RECEIVABLE with a credit, reflecting the reduction in this asset account and also reduce the ALLOWANCE FOR UNCOLLECTIBLES contra-account with a debit. As long as LCI has recognized enough UNCOLLECTIBLE EXPENSE in advance of the actual loss, accountants do not need to recognize any loss at the time that the company learns of actual losses.

5.2. Revisit the July 18 transaction described in Question 4.5. Now, the July 18 transaction must include the additional information provided in Question 5.1. You receive payment in full on July 18 for the June sales to OEM Communications. You pay the sales commission to Lavalier Sales and Marketing (Channel Islands) and keep the balance of the cash in your demand deposit account.

7/18/20X1	CASH	$91,000	
7/18/20X1	ACCOUNTS RECEIVABLE		$91,000
7/18/20X1	ACCOUNTS PAYABLE	$18,200	
7/18/20X1	CASH		$18,200

5.3. Recall in Question 1.6, you bought $45,000 of equipment on January 19. Your auditing firm advises you to use a four-year life, zero residual value and suggests you use the straight-line method of depreciation. Your auditor believes it is acceptable to treat the current year as a full year for depreciation purposes. Enter the depreciation entries for 20X1 as a once-a-year entry on December 31.

12/31/20X1	DEPRECIATION EXPENSE	$11,250	
12/31/20X1	ACCUMULATED DEPRECIATION		$11,250

When LCI bought the equipment, the company recognized no expense. To account for the gradual wear and tear of the equipment, the accountant creates an expense. The expense must be calculated because it is an accrual. That is, the amount is artificially created by accountants to spread the $45,000 cost over the useful life of the equipment.

The equipment is worthless after four years. Accountants use a number of ways to spread the decline in asset value but the question suggests that you should use the straight-line method. That method picks up $11,250 each year for four years (totaling $45,000).

The debit is an expense that resembles the expenses used by LCI in the previous questions. However, the accountants create the expense for the purpose of reflecting the wear and tear on the equipment and timing the expense to correspond to the time the equipment is in use.

The account credited reflects the decrease in the value of the equipment due to use. The accumulation account reduces the value of LCI assets by $11,250 on the company balance sheet. However, the way accountants reflect this loss in value is to create a contra-asset account. Notice that accountants do not adjust the value of the EQUIPMENT account. Instead, the loss in value is accumulated in the ACCUMULATED DEPRECIATION—EQUIPMENT account.

Accountants maintain separate accounts for the purchase cost of the equipment and the depreciation expense applied to the equipment. As a result, the balance sheet can reflect both the undepreciated cost of the equipment and the value reflecting the accumulated depreciation.

5.4. On January 4, you hire four employees (including yourself) for salaries totaling $600,000 per year, payable monthly. However, 20 percent of the salaries are withheld for payroll taxes.

1/31/20X1	SALARY EXPENSE	$40,000	
1/31/20X1	PAYROLL TAX EXPENSE	10,000	
1/31/20X1	CASH		40,000
1/31/20X1	PAYROLL TAXES PAYABLE		10,000
2/28/20X1	SALARY EXPENSE	40,000	
2/28/20X1	PAYROLL TAX EXPENSE	10,000	
2/28/20X1	CASH		40,000
2/28/20X1	PAYROLL TAXES PAYABLE		10,000
3/31/20X1	SALARY EXPENSE	40,000	
3/31/20X1	PAYROLL TAX EXPENSE	10,000	
3/31/20X1	CASH		40,000
3/31/20X1	PAYROLL TAXES PAYABLE		10,000

4/30/20X1	SALARY EXPENSE	40,000	
4/30/20X1	PAYROLL TAX EXPENSE	10,000	
4/30/20X1	CASH		40,000
4/30/20X1	PAYROLL TAXES PAYABLE		10,000
5/31/20X1	SALARY EXPENSE	40,000	
5/31/20X1	PAYROLL TAX EXPENSE	10,000	
5/31/20X1	CASH		40,000
5/31/20X1	PAYROLL TAXES PAYABLE		10,000
6/30/20X1	SALARY EXPENSE	40,000	
6/30/20X1	PAYROLL TAX EXPENSE	10,000	
6/30/20X1	CASH		40,000
6/30/20X1	PAYROLL TAXES PAYABLE		10,000
7/31/20X1	SALARY EXPENSE	40,000	
7/31/20X1	PAYROLL TAX EXPENSE	10,000	
7/31/20X1	CASH		40,000
7/31/20X1	PAYROLL TAXES PAYABLE		10,000
8/31/20X1	SALARY EXPENSE	40,000	
8/31/20X1	PAYROLL TAX EXPENSE	10,000	
8/31/20X1	CASH		40,000
8/31/20X1	PAYROLL TAXES PAYABLE		10,000
9/30/20X1	SALARY EXPENSE	40,000	
9/30/20X1	PAYROLL TAX EXPENSE	10,000	
9/30/20X1	CASH		40,000
9/30/20X1	PAYROLL TAXES PAYABLE		10,000
10/31/20X1	SALARY EXPENSE	40,000	
10/31/20X1	PAYROLL TAX EXPENSE	10,000	
10/31/20X1	CASH		40,000
10/31/20X1	PAYROLL TAXES PAYABLE		10,000
11/30/20X1	SALARY EXPENSE	40,000	
11/30/20X1	PAYROLL TAX EXPENSE	10,000	
11/30/20X1	CASH		40,000
11/30/20X1	PAYROLL TAXES PAYABLE		10,000
12/31/20X1	SALARY EXPENSE	40,000	
12/31/20X1	PAYROLL TAX EXPENSE	10,000	
12/31/20X1	CASH		40,000
12/31/20X1	PAYROLL TAXES PAYABLE		$10,000

This set of transactions greatly simplifies taxation. In fact, employers withhold for payroll tax, Social Security, unemployment, and state and federal income tax. Some of these taxes are paid at different rates, depending on income. Social Security tax is subject to a cap or maximum amount. Employers share the burden of payroll taxes, so that portion is not withheld but paid over and above the stated salary. To simplify the accounting entries, employees are paid a gross salary, but the employer withholds 20 percent and pays that amount quarterly (see below) to the government.

The company has an expense or several expenses associated with the staff it hires to conduct business. These entries presume that the taxes are deemed to be paid by the employer, so the out-of-pocket cost of $600,000 is broken into salary of $480,000 and tax of $120,000. If the tax were deemed to be paid by the employee, the accountant would probably record the entire $600,000 as a salary expense and the tax payment wouldn't be included on the income statement as a tax payment made by LCI.

Cash is leaving the firm at the rate of $40,000 per month, and a liability is growing by $10,000 per month. At the end of a quarter, the company will pay the tax, reducing the liability but also reducing cash by the amount of $10,000 per month. If LCI were on the cash basis, the accountants would recognize the monthly $40,000 expense when paid to the employees. However, the tax payment would not accrue at $10,000 per month. Instead, the company would recognize $30,000 each quarter when the cash is paid.

5.5. On each quarter end (March 31, June 30, September 30, and December 31), the company files payroll tax forms and pays the withheld taxes to the federal government (for simplicity, assume there is no state tax or company portion of payroll taxes).

3/31/20X1	PAYROLL TAXES PAYABLE	$30,000	
3/31/20X1	CASH		30,000
6/30/20X1	PAYROLL TAXES PAYABLE	30,000	
6/30/20X1	CASH		30,000
9/30/20X1	PAYROLL TAXES PAYABLE	30,000	
9/30/20X1	CASH		30,000
12/31/20X1	PAYROLL TAXES PAYABLE	30,000	
12/31/20X1	CASH		$30,000

It is important to explain why this series of transactions appears in Chapter 5, although they involve only balance sheet accounts. LCI created the liability because they accrue expenses. That is, in the set of transactions in Question 5.1, LCI recognized $10,000 in expense on 1/31/20X1 along with a payable. LCI posted the liability along with an accrued expense. Recall that accrued expenses are also temporary accounts, so they also reduce retained earnings by $10,000 per month. This debit (which appears as a debit to PAYROLL TAX EXPENSE) offsets a credit to the PAYROLL TAX PAYABLE account.

5.6. (*Note:* This question is presented out of sequence because the remaining questions are repetitious and hence presented in the section following.) You learn that Acme Electronics is in financial trouble. Acme owes you $288,750 for a sale on August 26. You agree to accept $242,000, which arrives on 10/15/X1.

Currently, you carry $25,564 in the ALLOWANCE FOR UNCOLLECTIBLES account.

10/15/20X1	CASH	$242,000	
10/15/20X1	UNCOLLECTIBLE EXPENSE	21,186	
10/15/20X1	ALLOWANCE FOR UNCOLLECTIBLES	25,564	
10/15/20X1	ACCOUNTS RECEIVABLE		$288,750

Presuming Acme actually pays the agreed amount of $242,000, cash goes up by that amount, which appears as a debit above. Likewise, the ACCOUNTS RECEIVABLE account goes down by $288,750 (a credit to an asset account) because LCI has agreed to accept $242,000 to satisfy the obligation. The difference between $288,750 and $242,000 equal to $46,750 is the amount that LCI must write off. If the ALLOWANCE FOR UNCOLLECTIBLES account held $46,750 or more, then accountants would have debited that account for the entire $46,750. Instead, the accountants must recognize an additional expense of $21,186 (debit as with other expenses).

LCI had been accruing expenses on previous trades with the intent of matching the timing of the credit losses to sales. As a new business without established customers and without a buildup to a balance in the allowance account, LCI has failed to match the timing of the write-off to the sales. As noted in questions below, LCI has decided to recognize an UNCOLLECTIBLE EXPENSE of 4 percent of all future sales.

5.7. To complete the year, you calculate the amortization on the patents acquired on January 19 for $2 million. You decide that the patents had 10 years of useful life remaining when acquired.

12/31/20X1	AMORTIZATION EXPENSE	$200,000	
12/31/20X1	PATENTS		$200,000

Note: The remaining questions and answers in Chapter 5 *reflect activities needed to describe sales that occur for the rest of the year. These questions and answers resemble transactions documented above.*

5.8. You sell 9,500 NCDs on July 25 to Excellent Acoustics for 25.75 against a cash payment in full. Lavalier Sales and Marketing (Channel Islands) was not involved in the transaction, so no commission is payable. Despite the advance payment, you decide to expense for uncollectibles anyway.

7/25/20X1	CASH	$244,625	
7/25/20X1	SALES REVENUE		244,625
7/25/20X1	UNCOLLECTIBLE EXPENSE	7,339	
7/25/20X1	ALLOWANCE FOR UNCOLLECTIBLES		7,339
7/25/20X1	COST OF GOODS SOLD	95,000	
7/25/20X1	FINISHED GOODS INVENTORY		95,000

This question follows the pattern above.

5.9. You sell 11,000 NCDs on August 26 to Acme Electronics for $26.25 for payment in 30 days. Lavalier Sales and Marketing (Channel Islands) was not involved in the transaction, so no commission is payable. You maintain a 3 percent allowance for uncollectibles.

8/26/20X1	ACCOUNTS RECEIVABLE	$288,750	
8/26/20X1	SALES REVENUE		288,750
8/26/20X1	UNCOLLECTIBLE EXPENSE	8,663	
8/26/20X1	ALLOWANCE FOR UNCOLLECTIBLES		8,663
8/26/20X1	COST OF GOODS SOLD	110,000	
8/26/20X1	FINISHED GOODS INVENTORY		$110,000

This question follows the pattern above.

5.10. You ship 9,500 NCDs on September 22 to OEM Communications for a gross price of $27.50 per unit to be paid within 30 days. A commission of 20 percent is payable to Lavalier Sales and Marketing (Channel Islands). Based on the prior experience of Lavalier Corporation, you predict that 3 percent of the sale is uncollectible.

9/22/20X1	ACCOUNTS RECEIVABLE	261,250	
9/22/20X1	SALES REVENUE		$261,250
9/22/20X1	COMMISSION EXPENSE	52,250	
9/22/20X1	ACCOUNTS PAYABLE		52,250
9/22/20X1	COST OF GOODS SOLD	95,000	
9/22/20X1	FINISHED GOODS INVENTORY		95,000
9/22/20X1	UNCOLLECTIBLE EXPENSE	7,838	
9/22/20X1	ALLOWANCE FOR UNCOLLECTIBLES		$ 7,838

5.11. You sell 10,000 NCDs on October 25 to Excellent Acoustics for $26 against a cash payment in full. Lavalier Sales and Marketing (Channel Islands) was not involved in the transaction, so no commission is payable. Despite the advance payment, you decide to expense for uncollectibles anyway. You decide to reserve 4 percent of sales as uncollectible from now on.

10/25/20X1	CASH	$260,000	
10/25/20X1	SALES REVENUE		260,000
10/25/20X1	COST OF GOODS SOLD	100,000	
10/25/20X1	FINISHED GOODS INVENTORY		100,000
10/25/20X1	UNCOLLECTIBLE EXPENSE	10,400	
10/25/20X1	ALLOWANCE FOR UNCOLLECTIBLES		$10,400

This question follows the pattern above.

5.12. You sell 10,000 NCDs on November 25 to Excellent Acoustics for 26 against a cash payment in full. Lavalier Sales and Marketing (Channel Islands) was not involved in the transaction, so no commission is payable. Despite the advance payment, you decide to expense for uncollectibles anyway. You reserve 4 percent of sales as uncollectible.

11/25/20X1	CASH	$260,000	
11/25/20X1	SALES REVENUE		260,000
11/25/20X1	COST OF GOODS SOLD	100,000	

11/25/20X1	FINISHED GOODS INVENTORY		100,000
11/25/20X1	UNCOLLECTIBLE EXPENSE	10,400	
11/25/20X1	ALLOWANCE FOR UNCOLLECTIBLES		$10,400

This question follows the pattern above.

5.13. You sell 11,000 NCDs on December 28 to Zebutronics Communications for $26.50 with payment due in 30 days. No commission is payable.

12/28/20X1	ACCOUNTS RECEIVABLE	$291,500	
12/28/20X1	SALES REVENUE		291,500
12/28/20X1	COST OF GOODS SOLD	110,000	
12/28/20X1	FINISHED GOODS INVENTORY		110,000
12/28/20X1	UNCOLLECTIBLE EXPENSE	11,660	
12/28/20X1	ALLOWANCE FOR UNCOLLECTIBLES		$11,660

5.14. On December 31, you receive the semiannual interest payment on the bond investment. You do not reinvest the interest from the December 31 payment in a new investment.

| 12/31/20X1 | CASH | $50,000 | |
| 12/31/20X1 | INTEREST REVENUE | | $50,000 |

This question follows the pattern above.

CHAPTER 6

6.1. Produce a statement of cash flows for Lavalier Communications, Inc. using the indirect method and the account totals from the trial balance below.

Statement of Cash Flows (Indirect), Lavalier Communications Inc. for the Year Ending December 31, 20X1

Cash Flows from Operating Activities	
Net income	$ 57,336
Adjustments to Reconcile Net Income to Net Cash Flows from Operating Activities	
Depreciation and amortization	$ 211,250
Noncash bad debt expenses	$33,465
Change in Current Assets and Current Liabilities	
Increase in accounts receivable	$ (291,500)
Increase in deposits	$ (4,000)
Increase in inventory	$ (5,000)
Increase in accounts payable	$ 100,000
Net cash flows from operating activities	$ 101,551
Cash Flow from Investing Activities	
Purchase equipment	$ (45,000)
Purchase bonds	$(2,000,000)
Purchase patents	$(2,000,000)
Net cash flow from investing activities	$(4,045,000)
Cash Flows from Financing Activities	
Proceeds from issuance of common stock	$ 5,000,000
Net cash inflow from financing activities	$ 5,000,000
Net increase in cash	$ 1,056,551
Cash balance, December 31, 20X1	$ 1,056,551
Cash balance, December 31, 20X0	$ 0

The statement of cash flows contains three sections. The first section documents cash flows from operations. The indirect method begins with net income, which for LCI was $57,336. The first set of adjustments adjusts from noncash expenses. LCI posted $200,000 amortization on the $2 million patents purchased and $11,250 on the equipment. The second noncash adjustment is to add back the $33,465 in the ALLOWANCE FOR uncollectibles. Next, the indirect statement adjusts for changes in current asset accounts on the balance sheet. In particular, the increase in accounts receivable, $391,500, uses that amount of cash; the security deposit with the landlord uses $4,000; and the year-end inventory uses $5,000, but the increase in accounts payable acts as a source of cash. Together, the company generated $101,551 cash from operations.

The second section of the indirect statement of cash flows measures the impact of investing on the cash balances of LCI. The investment in equipment used $45,000 in cash, the investment in bonds used $2 million, and the investment in patents used $2 million. Together, investing activities used $4,045,000.

The third section of the indirect statement of cash flows measures the impact of financing on the cash balances of LCI. The company issued $5 million is stock, providing that amount of cash to the company.

The net impact on LCI cash is the total of $101,551 provided by operations, $4,045,000 used in investing, and $5,000,000 provided by financing operations. The net impact is $1,056,551, which matches the ending cash balance. Because the company began with no cash, the statement reconciles to the cash on the balance sheet.

6.2. Produce a statement of cash flows for Lavalier Communications, Inc. using the direct method and the account totals from the trial balance below.

Statement of Cash Flows (Indirect), Lavalier Communications, Inc. for the Year Ending December 31, 20X1

Cash Flows from Operating Activities		
Cash Receipts		
From customers	$ 1,358,875	
Interest received	$ 131,126	$ 1,490,001
Cash payments		
To suppliers	$ 554,000	
For operating expenses	$ 834,450	$1,388,450
Net cash provided by		$ 101,551
operating activities		
Cash Flows from Investing Activities		
Purchase of equipment	$ (45,000)	
Purchase of patents	$(2,000,000)	
Increase in bond	$(2,000,000)	$(4,045,000)
investments		
Cash Flows from Financing Activities		
Issuance of common stock	$ 5,000,000	$ 5,000,000
Increase in cash		$ 1,056,551
Cash at beginning of period		$ 0
Cash at end of period		$ 1,056,551

The direct statement of cash flows also reviews the impact of operations, investing, and financing on cash balances. The operating section begins by calculating the cash receipts. The first amount is the net cash received from customers. This amount of $1,358,875 is the net of SALES REVENUES ($1,697,125) less the increase in ACCOUNTS RECEIVABLE ($291,500) less the UNCOLLECTIBLE ACCOUNTS EXPENSE ($80,215) plus the increase in the ALLOWANCE FOR UNCOLLECTIBLES ($33,465). The second source of cash is interest totaling $131,126. Together, cash receipts total $1,490,001.

The second section of the operating portion of the direct method statement of cash flows measures cash payments. Payments to suppliers ($554,000) equal the COST OF GOODS SOLD ($645,000) plus the increase in INVENTORY ($5,000) less the increase in ACCOUNTS PAYABLE ($100,000) plus the SECURITY DEPOSIT ($4,000). The next set of payments equals $834,450 of operating expenses, including salary ($480,000), payroll taxes ($120,000), commissions ($70,450), rent payments ($48,000), and patent license fees ($120,000). Together, the cash payments total $1,388,450.

The net of $1,490,001 cash receipts and $1,388,450 is $101,551 cash provided by operations. This cash provided by operations equals the cash provided by operations calculated using the indirect method.

The investing and financing sections are the same on both the direct and the indirect statement of cash flows. Therefore, the direct statement of cash flows also reconciles to the cash on the balance sheet of $1,056,551.

CHAPTER 7

7.1. Suppose LCI accountants have made several mistakes in entering some accounting transactions. The company determines that they entered a particular debit twice in January, entered a debit as a credit in March, and failed to enter anything for a business transaction in May. Should the company edit and correct the entries in the database?

Accountants would advise against altering past records. A better policy is to maintain systems that do not permit any kind of alterations to existing data. Errors do occur, but a better approach would be to (1) maintain the original error and (2) enter additional corrective entries to reverse and reenter the transactions properly.

These correcting entries should make it clear that these transactions are corrections and cross-reference to the original erroneous entries and ideally to documents supporting the correction.

7.2. The financial statements of two companies reveal that one company has made many accounting assumptions that have the effect of raising profitability. In contrast, the second company does not seem to have adopted accounting conventions that lead to higher profitability. How can you compare the financial statements of the two companies?

The companies must produce statements that are consistent from year to year or at least document how changes in accounting policy have affected the results. But generally accepted accounting methods allow enough flexibility that direct comparisons of the financial results may not be directly comparable.

Chapter 8 will introduce financial statement analysis. Investors and managers who carefully read the financial statements of companies can identify the ways in which a company made decisions that resulted in higher or lower earnings, larger or smaller assets, and whether accountants made decisions to make the reported financial results more consistent. Skillful analysts can also restate the financial results of companies to create more consistency between companies. These adjusted financial results permit more useful comparison of the statements of different companies.

7.3. How can a company ensure the integrity of their records if automated data entry has removed the "paper trail"?

Manual systems are susceptible to human error. Audit can identify whether the accounting records generally are accurate but cannot be certain that all errors have been detected. However, a vigilant audit should discourage attempts to create fraudulent accounting records inconsistent with the physical documents the company may produce. Automated systems are much less susceptible to error, and accountants can check to see if the software used behaves as expected.

Companies can preserve a trail, even when paper records are not preserved. Companies can preserve sales statistics, purchase requisitions, or other inputs to automated accounting systems outside the accounting ledger. This duplicate information provides an opportunity for modern auditors to follow a data trail or computer trail to verify the accuracy of company records.

Companies should also separate the duties, so that those individuals that are being measured are not responsible for creating the financial records that monitor their performance. Naturally, efforts to automate the data inputs also can separate individuals from the opportunity to manipulate accounting records.

CHAPTER 8

Note: For each of the financial ratios below, determine if you have enough information to calculate the ratio. Then calculate the ratio where possible and comment on conclusions that may be reached about Lavalier Communications, Inc. using this ratio.

8.1. Current ratio

$$\text{Current Ratio} = \frac{\text{Current Assets}}{\text{Current Liabilities}} = \frac{1,323,586}{100,000}$$

$$= 13.2 \text{ to } 1 \qquad (8.1)$$

The current ratio shows that LCI has considerable short-term liquidity. Companies often seek to keep their current assets about equal to the current liabilities (a current ratio of 1 to 1). In comparison, LCI appears to have excessive liquidity.

However, as a start-up company, LCI is prudent to keep adequate cash on hand. Many new businesses consume significant amounts of cash. LCI was fortunate to be able to get into business and begin making sales rapidly. After some significant initial cash outlays in investments, the company cash flow is positive. LCI is in a position to expand production and perhaps make the investment in production facilities, if in-house manufacture could be expected to lower costs or increase capacity.

8.2. Acid test or quick ratio

$$\text{Quick Ratio} = \frac{\text{Cash} + \text{Short-Term Investments} + \text{Accounts Receivables}}{\text{Current Liabilities}}$$

$$= \frac{1,056,551 + 0 + 258,035}{100,000}$$

$$= 13.1 \qquad (8.2)$$

The quick ratio is similar to the current ratio for most companies and nearly identical for LCI. The accounts receivable here is net of the allowance for uncollectibles.

As with the current ratio, LCI appears to have too much liquidity. As the company becomes confident in generating sufficient cash, managers can begin to use the existing cash and investments to invest in future growth.

8.3. Accounts receivable turnover

$$\text{Accounts Receivable Turnover} = \frac{\text{Net Credit Sales}}{\text{Average Net Accounts Receivable}}$$

$$\frac{932,500 - 80,215}{(0 + 258,035)/2} = 6.61 \tag{8.3}$$

The accounts receivable turnover is an unimpressive 6.61 times. This means that, on average, LCI took about two months to collect on a credit sale. The company made seven sales in 20X1. Four sales were credit sales totaling $932,500. The numerator reduces these credit sales by the accrued expense for uncollectible accounts rather than the actual loss experienced. The denominator averages beginning accounts receivables (zero) and ending accounts receivables net of the ALLOWANCE FOR UNCOLLECTIBLES.

The averaging of the denominator presents a fair view of the accounts receivable turnover. Next year, if ACCOUNTS RECEIVABLES holds steady at year-end levels, then the ratio would decline to 3.30. However, it is reasonable to believe that credit sales in the numerator would also be about twice as high. Unless performance changes, the accounts receivable turnover should be about the same next year.

The company should look to collect more rapidly. While the company currently has plenty of cash to finance the accounts receivable, it leaves the company exposed to credit losses and uses cash that could be used to expand the business.

8.4. Days' sales in receivables

$$\text{Days' Sales in Receivables} = \frac{\text{Average Net Accounts Receivable}}{\text{One Day's Sales}}$$

$$\frac{258,035/2}{1,697,125/365} = 27.7 \text{ days} \tag{8.4}$$

This ratio is considerably more favorable than the accounts receivable turnover ratio. The accounts receivable balance is reduced by the amount in the UNCOLLECTIBLE ALLOWANCE account and averaged with a zero starting level. Daily sales equals annual sales divided by 365. The resulting ratio suggests that LCI has been collecting in less than a month. This result is more consistent with an inspection of the individual trades.

8.5. Inventory turnover

$$\text{Inventory Turnover} = \frac{\text{Cost of Goods Sold}}{\text{Average Inventory}}$$

$$\frac{645,000}{5,000/2} = 258 \tag{8.5}$$

The inventory turnover ratio is a very impressive 258 to 1. Probably, this turnover ratio will decline as the company grows. But the company was left with a small amount of inventory at year-end.

Reviewing the individual transactions suggests that the very favorable performance of LCI in turning over their inventory is realistic. Most months, the company sold roughly their entire monthly production shortly after receiving inventory. As a result, the company generally held very little inventory.

The company should focus on finding ways to increase production and see if they can increase sales if they have adequate inventory on hand all month long. If necessary, the company should consider investing in plant and equipment to increase the units available for sale and to possibly reduce the cost of production.

8.6. Return on assets

$$\text{Return on Assets} = \frac{\text{Net Income} + \text{Interest Expense}}{\text{Average Total Assets}}$$

$$\frac{57,336 + 0}{5,157,336/2} = 2.2\% \tag{8.6}$$

The company did not produce much profit, so return on assets is fairly low. Still, for a start-up company to be profitable in the first year is impressive. The company needs to expand sales to earn the gross margin on a large amount of sales.

8.7. Return on equity

$$\text{Return on Equity} = \frac{\text{Net Income} - \text{Preferred Dividends}}{\text{Average Equity}}$$

$$\frac{57,336}{(0 + 5,057,336)/2} = 2.27\% \text{ or}$$

$$\frac{57,336}{(5,000,000 + 5,057,336)/2} = 1.14\% \tag{8.7}$$

LCI has issued no preferred stock, so it paid no preferred dividends. The formula calls for calculating average equity, which includes the $5 million of capital contributed by Lavalier Corporation plus the retained earnings for 20X1. The formula averages beginning and ending capital. This average would ordinarily reflect $0 capital at the previous year-end averaged with $5,057,336. By this measure, the company earned a 2.27 percent return on equity.

However, the company had $5 million from the second day of the year plus earnings, which the company earned in the second half of the year. A second measure averaged $5 million with $5,057,336 to produce a return on equity of only 1.14 percent.

In fact, neither ratio is high enough to please the investors. Established companies earn 10 to 15 percent on equity. Technology companies often earn much higher returns. Lavalier Corporation could expect to earn higher returns by investing in other companies earning a market return.

However, 20X1 was the first year that LCI was in business. In fact, it was making retail sales only in the second half of the year. Lavalier Corporation should be pleased to make a profit on its investment in LCI in the first year of operation.

LCI has plenty of cash and seems to be on the way to becoming a successful company. The company will benefit from a full year of sales and may be able to increase sales. LCI should improve profitability by increasing unit sales, find ways to lower costs, and consider raising prices.

8.8. Gross profit percentage

$$\text{Gross Profit Percentage} = \frac{\text{Gross Profit}}{\text{Net Sales Revenue}}$$

$$\frac{\text{Sales} - \text{Cost of Goods Sold}}{\text{Sales}} = \frac{1{,}697{,}125 - 645{,}000}{1{,}697{,}125}$$

$$= 61.99\% \tag{8.8}$$

With the benefit of patent protection, LCI is earning an attractive 61.99 percent gross profit percentage. Technology companies often earn high margins, so this ratio suggests that the company is pricing the product in line with industry patterns.

The high gross profit percentage demonstrates that LCI is making returns on sales but needs to increase sales to cover fixed costs, such as salaries and patent costs.

8.9. Profit margin

$$\text{Profit Margin} = \text{Return on Sales} = \frac{\text{Net Income}}{\text{Net Sales}}$$

$$\frac{57{,}336}{1{,}697{,}125} = 3.38\% \tag{8.9}$$

The profit margin is low because net income is low. As mentioned above, the company should be pleased to be profitable in the first year of operation. For the same reason, it is not reasonable to expect to earn a competitive profit margin immediately. Because the gross profit is satisfactory, the low profit margin is not a concern at this time.

8.10. Asset turnover

$$\text{Asset Turnover} = \frac{\text{Net Sales}}{\text{Average Total Assets}}$$

$$\frac{1,697,125}{(0 + 5,157,336)/2} = 65.81\%$$

$$\frac{2*1,697,125}{(5,000,000 + 5,157,336)/2} = 66.83\% \qquad (8.10)$$

The sales in the ratio come from the second half of the year. For this reason, it seems logical to also reduce the total assets as suggested by the standard textbook formula. In fact, it may make sense to roughly double the sales to reflect an entire year of operation and divide that amount by the average assets beginning around January 2. This alternative does not significantly change the ratio because both the numerator and the denominator are roughly double.

Asset turnover varies widely from industry to industry. Analysts would want to compare LCI's asset turnover to other communications companies.

Companies with a higher profit margin can earn a fair return on lower turnover. LCI has not started to earn high profits, but insiders can expect to see dramatic improvement as the company matures.

8.11. Earnings per share

$$\text{EPS} = \frac{\text{Net Income} - \text{Preferred Dividends}}{\text{Weighted Average Shares Outstanding}}$$

$$\frac{\$57,336}{1,000,000} = \$.06 \qquad (8.11)$$

LCI issued 1 million shares to Lavalier very near the beginning of 20X1, so 1 million shares is used above. The net income for the company divided by the number of shares produces earnings of just under $.06 per share.

Investors track earnings per share over time to get a fair measure of growth in financial success. If the company issues more shares, then rising earnings don't necessarily translate into higher per share earnings.

8.12. Fully diluted EPS

$$\text{Fully Diluted EPS} = \frac{\text{Net Income} - \text{Preferred Dividends}}{\text{Total Shares Potentially Outstanding}}$$

$$\frac{\$57,336}{1,200,000} = .05 \tag{8.12}$$

The company has granting options on 200,000 shares (see Question 1.2). If the shares are exercised, the company will issue 200,000 additional shares and have 1,200,000 shares outstanding. The fully diluted earnings per share divides the net income less preferred dividends (LCI has no preferred dividends) by 1.2 million shares.

8.13. Debt ratio

$$\text{Debt Ratio} = \text{Debt to Total Assets} = \frac{\text{Total Liabilities}}{\text{Total Assets}}$$

$$\frac{100,000}{5,157,336} = \text{near zero} \tag{8.13}$$

The company has no debt except for $100,000 trade credit representing the most recent delivery of inventory. As a result, the debt ratio is very close to zero.

Many companies, especially technology companies, have little or no debt. LCI also has no reason to issue debt at the present. The company has over $1 million in cash and an additional $2 million in medium-term investments. The company has the money to make substantial investments without borrowing.

Based on the ratios reviewed so far, LCI should be able to borrow money if profitable investments justify taking on the debt. The coupon rate on new debt for LCI would be high because the company has been in business for only a year. However, as the company builds a track record, LCI has the opportunity to grow by issuing debt and investing in new operating assets.

8.14. Debt-to-equity ratio

$$\text{Debt to Equity} = \frac{\text{Total Debt}}{\text{Total Equity}}$$

$$\frac{100,000}{5,057,336} = \text{near zero} \tag{8.14}$$

The debt-to-equity ratio is just above zero because LCI has no debt except for 100,000 trade credit for the latest shipment of NCDs. This ratio should be interpreted similar to the debt ratio above.

8.15. Times interest earned

$$\text{Times Interest Earned} = \frac{\text{Operating Income}}{\text{Interest Expense}} \tag{8.15}$$

The company has no borrowings that require LCI to pay interest. As a result, the interest expense is zero. It is impossible to calculate this ratio.

8.16. Book value per share

$$\text{Book Value} = \frac{\text{Shareholders' Equity} - \text{Preferred Equity}}{\text{Common Shares Outstanding}}$$

$$\frac{5{,}057{,}336}{1{,}000{,}000} = 5.06 \tag{8.16}$$

The company has no preferred equity. The book value per share equals the initial paid-in cost of \$5 per share plus the \$.06 per share earned in 20X1.

8.17. Price-earnings ratio

$$\text{P/E} = \frac{\text{Market Price per Share}}{\text{EPS}} \tag{8.17}$$

Since shares of LCI are not publicly traded, no market price is available. It might be possible to substitute an appraised value, but there is no evidence that the shares have been valued for anyone since they were issued on January 2, 20X1, at least a year ago. As a result, it is not possible to calculate a P/E ratio for LCI.

8.18. Dividend yield

$$\text{Dividend Yield} = \frac{\text{Dividend per Share}}{\text{Market Price per Share}}$$

$$= \frac{0}{\text{Market Price}} \tag{8.18}$$

The market price is not known for LCI. However, it is still possible to calculate the dividend yield in this particular case because 0 divided by any price is a yield of zero. Stated as a math problem, this seems to be a trick question. Yet if you heard that a company paid no dividend, you would probably conclude that the dividend yield is zero without checking the stock price.

8.19. Payout ratio

$$\text{Payout Ratio} = \frac{\text{Cash Dividends}}{\text{Net Income}} = \frac{0}{57{,}336} \tag{8.19}$$

The scenarios in these homework questions mentioned no dividend payment. Therefore, the dividend payout ratio is 0 or 0 percent.

The company could have declared a dividend up to almost $.06 per share. In many cases, companies can pay dividends only from retained earnings, and this new company has only earnings from 20X1.

Suppose that the company declared a dividend of $.03 per share some time in 20X1. Then the payout ratio would be $30,000/ $57,336, or 52 percent.

GENERAL JOURNAL FOR COLLECTED QUESTIONS

1.	1/2/20X1	CASH	5,000,000	
	1/2/20X1	COMMON STOCK		1,000,000
	1/2/20X1	PAID-IN CAPITAL IN EXCESS OF PAR		4,000,000
2.	1/2/20X1	No debit is required		
	1/2/20X1	No credit is required		
3.	1/2/20X1	INVESTMENT IN BONDS	2,000,000	
	1/2/20X1	CASH		2,000,000
4.	1/2/20X1	PATENTS	2,000,000	
	1/2/20X1	CASH		2,000,000
5.	1/31/20X1	SALARY EXPENSE	40,000	
	1/31/20X1	PAYROLL TAX EXPENSE	10,000	
	1/31/20X1	CASH		40,000
	1/31/20X1	PAYROLL TAXES PAYABLE		10,000
	2/28/20X1	SALARY EXPENSE	40,000	
	2/28/20X1	PAYROLL TAX EXPENSE	10,000	
	2/28/20X1	CASH		40,000
	2/28/20X1	PAYROLL TAXES PAYABLE		10,000
	3/31/20X1	SALARY EXPENSE	40,000	
	3/31/20X1	PAYROLL TAX EXPENSE	10,000	
	3/31/20X1	CASH		40,000
	3/31/20X1	PAYROLL TAXES PAYABLE		10,000
	4/30/20X1	SALARY EXPENSE	40,000	
	4/30/20X1	PAYROLL TAX EXPENSE	10,000	
	4/30/20X1	CASH		$40,000
	4/30/20X1			10,000

	PAYROLL TAXES PAYABLE		
5/31/20X1	SALARY EXPENSE	40,000	
5/31/20X1	PAYROLL TAX EXPENSE	10,000	
5/31/20X1	CASH		40,000
5/31/20X1	PAYROLL TAXES PAYABLE		10,000
6/30/20X1	SALARY EXPENSE	40,000	
6/30/20X1	PAYROLL TAX EXPENSE	10,000	
6/30/20X1	CASH		40,000
6/30/20X1	PAYROLL TAXES PAYABLE		10,000
7/31/20X1	SALARY EXPENSE	40,000	
7/31/20X1	PAYROLL TAX EXPENSE	10,000	
7/31/20X1	CASH		40,000
7/31/20X1	PAYROLL TAXES PAYABLE		10,000
8/31/20X1	SALARY EXPENSE	40,000	
8/31/20X1	PAYROLL TAX EXPENSE	10,000	
8/31/20X1	CASH		40,000
8/31/20X1	PAYROLL TAXES PAYABLE		10,000
9/30/20X1	SALARY EXPENSE	40,000	
9/30/20X1	PAYROLL TAX EXPENSE	10,000	
9/30/20X1	CASH		40,000
9/30/20X1	PAYROLL TAXES PAYABLE		10,000
10/31/20X1	SALARY EXPENSE	40,000	
10/31/20X1	PAYROLL TAX EXPENSE	10,000	
10/31/20X1	CASH		40,000
10/31/20X1	PAYROLL TAXES PAYABLE		10,000
11/30/20X1	SALARY EXPENSE	40,000	
11/30/20X1	PAYROLL TAX EXPENSE	10,000	
11/30/20X1	CASH		40,000
11/30/20X1	PAYROLL TAXES PAYABLE		10,000
12/31/20X1	SALARY EXPENSE	40,000	
12/31/20X1	PAYROLL TAX EXPENSE	10,000	
12/31/20X1	CASH		40,000
12/31/20X1	PAYROLL TAXES PAYABLE		10,000
6. 3/31/20X1	PAYROLL TAXES PAYABLE	30,000	
3/31/20X1	CASH		30,000

	6/30/20X1	PAYROLL TAXES PAYABLE	30,000	
	6/30/20X1	CASH		30,000
	9/30/20X1	PAYROLL TAXES PAYABLE	30,000	
	9/30/20X1	CASH		30,000
	12/31/20X1	PAYROLL TAXES PAYABLE	30,000	
	12/31/20X1	CASH		30,000
7.	1/16/20X1	SECURITY DEPOSITS	4,000	
	1/16/20X1	PREPAID RENT	4,000	
	1/16/20X1	CASH		8,000
	2/1/20X1	RENT EXPENSE	4,000	
	2/1/20X1	PREPAID RENT		4,000
	3/1/20X1	RENT EXPENSE	4,000	
	3/1/20X1	CASH		4,000
	4/1/20X1	RENT EXPENSE	4,000	
	4/1/20X1	CASH		4,000
	5/1/20X1	RENT EXPENSE	4,000	
	5/1/20X1	CASH		4,000
	6/1/20X1	RENT EXPENSE	4,000	
	6/1/20X1	CASH		4,000
	7/1/20X1	RENT EXPENSE	4,000	
	7/1/20X1	CASH		4,000
	8/1/20X1	RENT EXPENSE	4,000	
	8/1/20X1	CASH		4,000
	9/1/20X1	RENT EXPENSE	4,000	
	9/1/20X1	CASH		4,000
	10/1/20X1	RENT EXPENSE	4,000	
	10/1/20X1	CASH		4,000
	11/1/20X1	RENT EXPENSE	4,000	
	11/1/20X1	CASH		4,000
	12/1/20X1	RENT EXPENSE	4,000	
	12/1/20X1	CASH		4,000
8.	1/19/20X1	EQUIPMENT	45,000	
	1/19/20X1	ACCOUNTS PAYABLE		45,000
	2/27/20X1	ACCOUNTS PAYABLE	45,000	
	2/27/20X1	CASH		45,000
	12/31/20X1	DEPRECIATION EXPENSE	11,250	
	12/31/20X1	ACCUMULATED DEPRECIATION		11,250
9.	1/28/20X1	ADVANCES TO SUPPLIERS	250,000	
	1/28/20X1	CASH		250,000
10.	3/31/20X1	PATENT LICENSE EXPENSE	30,000	
	3/31/20X1	CASH		30,000

6/30/20X1	PATENT LICENSE EXPENSE	30,000	
6/30/20X1	CASH		30,000
9/30/20X1	PATENT LICENSE EXPENSE	30,000	
9/30/20X1	CASH		30,000
12/31/20X1	PATENT LICENSE EXPENSE	30,000	
12/31/20X1	CASH		30,000
11. 6/19/20X1	FINISHED GOODS INVENTORY	50,000	
6/19/20X1	ADVANCES TO SUPPLIERS		50,000
12. 6/22/20X1	ACCOUNTS RECEIVABLE	91,000	
6/22/20X1	SALES REVENUE		91,000
6/22/20X1	COMMISSION EXPENSE	18,200	
6/22/20X1	ACCOUNTS PAYABLE		18,200
6/22/20X1	COST OF GOODS SOLD	35,000	
6/22/20X1	FINISHED GOODS INVENTORY		35,000
6/22/20X1	UNCOLLECTIBLE EXPENSE	2,730	
6/22/20X1	ALLOWANCE FOR UNCOLLECTIBLES		2,730
13. 6/30/20X1	CASH	50,000	
6/30/20X1	INTEREST REVENUE		50,000
14. 7/18/20X1	CASH	91,000	
7/18/20X1	ACCOUNTS RECEIVABLE		91,000
7/18/20X1	ACCOUNTS PAYABLE	18,200	
7/18/20X1	CASH		18,200
15. 7/23/20X1	FINISHED GOODS INVENTORY	100,000	
7/23/20X1	ADVANCES TO SUPPLIERS		100,000
16. 7/25/20X1	CASH	244,625	
7/25/20X1	SALES REVENUE		244,625
7/25/20X1	UNCOLLECTIBLE EXPENSE	7,339	
7/25/20X1	ALLOWANCE FOR UNCOLLECTIBLES		7,339
7/25/20X1	COST OF GOODS SOLD	95,000	
7/25/20X1	FINISHED GOODS INVENTORY		95,000
17. 8/22/20X1	FINISHED GOODS INVENTORY	100,000	
8/22/20X1			100,000

		ADVANCES TO SUPPLIERS		
18.	8/26/20X1	ACCOUNTS RECEIVABLE	288,750	
	8/26/20X1	SALES REVENUE		288,750
	8/26/20X1	UNCOLLECTIBLE EXPENSE	8,663	
	8/26/20X1	ALLOWANCE FOR UNCOLLECTIBLES		8,663
	8/26/20X1	COST OF GOODS SOLD	110,000	
	8/26/20X1	FINISHED GOODS INVENTORY		110,000
19.	9/19/20X1	FINISHED GOODS INVENTORY	100,000	
	9/19/20X1	ACCOUNTS PAYABLE		100,000
	9/26/20X1	ACCOUNTS PAYABLE	100,000	
	9/26/20X1	CASH		100,000
20.	9/22/20X1	ACCOUNTS RECEIVABLE	261,250	
	9/22/20X1	SALES REVENUE		261,250
	9/22/20X1	COMMISSION EXPENSE	52,250	
	9/22/20X1	ACCOUNTS PAYABLE		52,250
	9/22/20X1	COST OF GOODS SOLD	95,000	
	9/22/20X1	FINISHED GOODS INVENTORY		95,000
	9/22/20X1	UNCOLLECTIBLE EXPENSE	7,838	
	9/22/20X1	ALLOWANCE FOR UNCOLLECTIBLES		7,838
21.	10/15/20X1	CASH	242,000	
	10/15/20X1	ALLOWANCE FOR UNCOLLECT.	25,564	
	10/15/20X1	UNCOLLECTIBLE EXPENSE	21,186	
	10/15/20X1	ACCOUNTS RECEIVABLE		288,750
22.	10/21/20X1	CASH	261,250	
	10/21/20X1	ACCOUNTS RECEIVABLE		261,250
	10/21/20X1	ACCOUNTS PAYABLE	52,250	
	10/21/20X1	CASH		52,250
23.	10/22/20X1	FINISHED GOODS INVENTORY	100,000	
	10/22/20X1	CASH		100,000
24.	10/25/20X1	CASH	260,000	
	10/25/20X1	SALES REVENUE		260,000
	10/25/20X1	COST OF GOODS SOLD	100,000	
	10/25/20X1	FINISHED GOODS INVENTORY		100,000
	10/25/20X1	UNCOLLECTIBLE EXPENSE	10,400	

	10/25/20X1	ALLOWANCE FOR UNCOLLECTIBLES		10,400
25.	11/21/20X1	FINISHED GOODS INVENTORY	100,000	
	11/21/20X1	CASH		100,000
26.	11/25/20X1	CASH	260,000	
	11/25/20X1	SALES REVENUE		260,000
	11/25/20X1	COST OF GOODS SOLD	100,000	
	11/25/20X1	FINISHED GOODS INVENTORY		100,000
	11/25/20X1	UNCOLLECTIBLE EXPENSE	10,400	
	11/25/20X1	ALLOWANCE FOR UNCOLLECTIBLES		10,400
27.	11/21/20X1	FINISHED GOODS INVENTORY	100,000	
	11/21/20X1	ACCOUNTS PAYABLE		100,000
28.	12/28/20X1	ACCOUNTS RECEIVABLE	291,500	
	12/28/20X1	SALES REVENUE		291,500
	12/28/20X1	COST OF GOODS SOLD	110,000	
	12/28/20X1	FINISHED GOODS INVENTORY		110,000
	12/28/20X1	UNCOLLECTIBLE EXPENSE	11,660	
	12/28/20X1	ALLOWANCE FOR UNCOLLECTIBLES		11,660
29.	12/31/20X1	CASH	50,000	
	12/31/20X1	INTEREST REVENUE		50,000
30.	12/31/20X1	AMORTIZATION EXPENSE	200,000	
	12/31/20X1	PATENTS		200,000
31.	12/31/20X1	CASH	31,126	
	12/31/20X1	INTEREST REVENUE		31,126
		Total Debits and Credits	14,507,429	14,507,429

About the Author

Stuart McCrary is a principal at Chicago Partners, a subsidiary of Navigant Consulting, Inc. Chicago Partners is an economic consulting company involved with forensic accounting, business valuation, securities valuation, labor, antitrust, and other economic issues. Mr. McCrary is involved with business valuation, securities valuation, and securities market practices.

Mr. McCrary teaches finance and accounting in the Master of Product Development Program, an executive master's program at Northwestern University's Robert R. McCormick School of Engineering and Applied Science. Mr. McCrary has also taught classes on hedge fund management and alternative investments at DePaul University's Charles H. Kellstadt Graduate School of Business. In addition, Mr. McCrary has taught classes in options and financial engineering at the Illinois Institute of Technology.

Mr. McCrary graduated from Northwestern University's Kellogg School of Management with a master's degree in business administration and from Northwestern University's Judd A. and Marjorie Weinberg School of Arts and Sciences with a bachelor of arts degree.

Index